Around the
Great Western Railway Then & Now

Around the
Great Western
Railway Then & Now

Laurence Waters

Contents

Half title page:

Blaenau Ffestiniog

Blaenau Ffestiniog was served by two separate lines: the GWR branch from Bala and the LNWR branch from Llandudno Junction. On 1 September 1958, '7400' class 0-6-0PT No 7409 waits at Blaenau Ffestiniog Central with the 2.20pm service to Bala. This line was closed to passengers on 4 January 1960 and today services to Blaenau use the old LNWR route but terminate at the old GWR station. It was not until April 1964 that a connecting line was laid to link the two stations which were either side of the town.

Blaenau Ffestiniog is now an interchange station with the narrow gauge Ffestiniog Railway to Porthmadog. This means it is now possible to do a round trip, using Shrewsbury as a base. One could travel to Minffordd or Porthmadog via the ex-Cambrian line, then on the narrow gauge to Blaenau and depart via the ex-LNWR route back to Shrewsbury via Llandudno Junction, the North Wales coast and Crewe. On 17 July 2001, Class 153 No 153363 waits to depart with the 11.45 First North Western service to Llandudno Junction. *GW Trust/David Heath*

Title page:

Wiveliscombe

The 4.3pm service from Taunton to Barnstaple departs from Wiveliscombe on 22 August 1964, hauled by '4300' class 2-6-0 No 7303. The 43-mile branch, which left the Bristol & Exeter main line at Norton Fitzwarren Junction, was opened through to Barnstaple on 1 November 1873. Built by the Devon & Somerset Railway, it was operated from the start by the Bristol & Exeter Railway. Passenger services between Taunton and Barnstaple were withdrawn on 3 October 1966 and Wiveliscombe was closed on the same date.

Today, the site is the headquarters of Mike Stacey (Builders) and a large office building covers the trackbed at this point. However, the old station building and goods shed survive and are used for storage, as seen here on 18 September 2001. *M. J. Fox/Peter Triggs*

This edition published in 2009 by Heathfield Railway Publications
A division of Eagle Editions Ltd
11 Heathfield
Royston
Herts, SG8 5BW
United Kingdom

Front cover:
Oxford. *GW Trust/Author*

Back cover upper:
Carmarthen. *GW Trust/G. Wright*

Back cover lower:
Acton main line. *GW Trust/Author*

ISBN: 978-1-906974-06-0

Introduction

It is now almost eight years since I produced the first volume of *The Great Western Then & Now*. In that time, considerable changes have taken place on Britain's railways, with privatisation resulting in the establishment of the various train operating companies, some more successful than others. The railway today is constantly evolving and even as I write, Wales & West has split into two new franchises: Wessex Trains and Wales & Borders.

A number of new stations have been opened, usually with some local authority support. The most contentious issue, however, was the privatisation of Railtrack. I was of the opinion that this part of the infrastructure should have remained in the public domain, and at the time of writing this is under review.

Although the book is titled *Around the Great Western Railway Then & Now*, it has proved impossible to find enough pre-1948 pictures showing something other than a train or single locomotive, which have not been published before. The essence of a book like this is to illustrate a station, junction or yard as it was and then try to re-create the scene as it is today. Unfortunately, many photographers chose to take their pictures of locomotives and trains on open expanses of track — not particularly interesting to re-create.

As the Great Western did not alter very much in the years immediately after Nationalisation I have therefore been able to use many illustrations from the 1950s. I have tried, where possible, to use photographs that have not been published before. In many cases, at locations where the line is still in operation, I have deliberately excluded a train so that the new photograph shows what survives. On a number of occasions I have also widened the view to give a better overall impression of what the scene looks like today. Readers of the first book will notice that I have revisited a few of the locations which were used then. This is to show more recent alterations, or because another old photograph from a different angle has become available.

It has been great fun producing this book. It really is amazing to turn up at a location that lost its railway 30-40 years ago and find platforms, buildings and other artefacts still in situ. Some locations have proved elusive; on a rather foggy morning I was unable to find Wolfhall Junction, and the sites of Sparkford and St Anne's Park, Bristol were impossible to reach without trespassing on the railway.

I would like to thank my colleague Bill Turner, who was my map reader on a number of trips. We did not get lost too often.

For the various locations in the Welsh valleys I had the kind assistance of Alun Powell and Islwyn Richards. Their spot-on guidance and knowledge of many sites saved a considerable amount of time and allowed many more locations to be visited. Much of the background information has been obtained from my own personal files and also the Great Western Trust Historic Archive at Didcot Railway Centre, and the Signalling Record Society. R. A. Cooke's Great Western track diagrams have again proved to be an accurate source of information.

Special thanks go to fellow photographers David Burns, Tony Doyle, Peter and David Heath, Peter Triggs and Geoff Wright, for covering some outlying areas for me. Also to Hugh Ballantyne, R. A. Cooke, J. Crockford, Larry Crosier, Phil Kelley, Doug Nichols, Alun Powell and Peter Webber for additional information, and finally to Peter Bowell for checking the text.

A large percentage of the 'then' photographs in this book are from the cameras of the late Peter Fry, Charles Gordon Stuart and Mark Yarwood, and are held in the Great Western Trust Collection at Didcot. Those from other sources are credited individually.

Laurence Waters
Oxford
February 2002

Paddington

This excellent view of Paddington was taken on 20 June 1908. Standing at Platforms 4 and 5 are special trains conveying guests to the King's garden party at Windsor Castle. On the left is Great Western 'County' class 4-4-0 No 3475 *County of Wilts* and on the right, De Glehn Compound 4-4-2 No 104 *Alliance*.

In November 1968, the platforms were shortened by extending the 'Lawn' about 40yd westward, and during the last couple of years this area has seen further development with a new mezzanine area and additional shops and fast-food outlets. Part of the refurbished Lawn area can be seen in this picture, taken from the mezzanine on 15 July 2001. *GW Trust/Author*

The Great Western Railway

The Great Western Railway, which was formed in 1835, opened its first section of line from Paddington to Maidenhead to passengers on 4 June 1838. These services were extended through to Bristol just three years later on 30 June 1841; from Paddington to Exeter via Bristol in May 1844; to Plymouth in May 1848; and with the opening of the Royal Albert Bridge at Saltash, to Penzance in May 1859.

South Wales was reached in 1851 with services running via Swindon, Gloucester and Chepstow. The first section of the South Wales main line was opened between Swindon and Gloucester in May 1845, and it was extended to Chepstow in September 1851. At Chepstow, the GWR connected with the South Wales Railway which had itself opened between Swansea and Chepstow in June 1850. The line was gradually extended westward as far as Neyland in April 1856. However, it did not reach Fishguard Harbour until August 1906.

The Great Western began serving the Midlands with the opening of the Oxford Railway in June 1844 and it was extended to Banbury in October 1850, to Birmingham in October 1852 and Wolverhampton in November 1854.

To many, the letters GWR meant the 'great way round', and not without good cause. The South West was reached via Bristol; South Wales via Gloucester; and Birmingham via Oxford. To address this problem new cut-off routes, to speed up services and shorten journey times, were opened between Wootton Bassett and Patchway in May 1903. This new direct route to Wales was made possible with the opening of the Severn Tunnel in December 1886. Services to the South West were also speeded up with the opening of another new 'cut-off', between Patney and Cogload in April 1906, and yet another from Ashendon to Aynho in July 1910.

The Grouping in 1923 saw the Great Western expand even further with the absorption of 32 independent companies. Almost overnight its route mileage increased from 3,026 to 3,804. Its total mileage including sidings rose from 6,645 to 8,993. The Great Western Railway was also the only major company to retain its identity after the 1923 Grouping, while Nationalisation of the railways in 1948 saw the GWR become British Railways Western Region. Of the Big Four companies the Great Western was the only one to retain its locomotive numbering system after Nationalisation.

At first there was little change, but the modernisation programmes of the 1950s and 1960s resulted in the elimination of steam traction. Widespread closures of secondary routes and branch lines, together with regional boundary changes in 1963, decimated the system. By 1985, the 150th anniversary of the old company, the route mileage had fallen to about 1,900, of which about 400 were for freight only.

By the early 1990s, the railways in this country were in a poor state, with years of under-investment having allowed the infrastructure to deteriorate. The effective denationalisation on 1 April 1994, and subsequent privatisation, is seeing considerable investment being made, particularly in many parts of the old Great Western system. It seems that at last the government and public alike are now realising that rail travel can be a viable alternative to the car.

Paddington

Paddington station *c*1913 with Great Western 'Duke' class 4-4-0 No 3258 *The Lizard* waiting to depart with a mixed train. It was during this period that the station layout was extensively altered to provide 12 platforms. Additional arrival platforms were provided and covered with a new overall roof, built in the same style as the original 1854 design.

During the 1930s, the station was again enlarged and the old wooden platforms were rebuilt in brick and paved. At the same time they were lengthened and were partially covered with new awnings, as seen here in this present-day picture, in which HSTs still dominate First Great Western main line services. *GW Trust/Author*

Paddington

The train shed at Paddington, c1910. Notice the wooden platforms and the early pattern globe electric lights. Electric lighting was first installed at Paddington during 1881. The large clock, a feature of Platform 1, was installed in 1903.

As already mentioned, Paddington has seen much refurbishment and modernisation in recent years to bring it into the 21st century. *GW Trust/Author*

Berkshire, Buckinghamshire, Hampshire, Oxfordshire and Middlesex

Since privatisation, services in the Home Counties have been operated by Thames Trains, Chiltern Railways, First Great Western and Virgin CrossCountry. There have been no line closures since Volume 1 was produced, and in many cases it has been a story of success and a greatly increased investment. Passenger services still operate over the Windsor, Henley, Marlow and Aylesbury branches, but others, including Abingdon, Fairford, Staines, Woodstock and Uxbridge, have gone for ever.

The Great Western main line out of Paddington station continues to be as busy as ever and with the introduction of the Heathrow Express electrified services on 23 June 1998, lines in this area have probably reached saturation point. Paddington itself has undergone another facelift with a new mezzanine area containing shops and cafés, built on the site of the old 'Lawn' area.

The cut-off route to Banbury, opened by the Great Western in 1910, has in recent years seen considerable investment by Chiltern Railways. Double track has now been reinstated between Aynho Junction, Bicester and Princes Risborough where the down platform has been brought back into use, and services now operate from Marylebone through to Birmingham Snow Hill. Investment has not been confined to stations and track. A new batch of 'Clubman' Class 168 DMUs was purchased especially for the Birmingham services and during May 2001, a number of these weekday services were running through to Stourbridge Junction.

First Great Western main line passenger services are still in the hands of HSTs, while Thames Valley local services from Paddington are operated by Thames Trains using Class 165 and 166 DMUs. Many of these trains are being refurbished and repainted in the new Thames Trains livery and provide what is essentially a half-hourly

interval service throughout the day. Chiltern Railways services to and from Marylebone are operated with Class 165 and 168 units. Virgin CrossCountry, at the time of writing, was using a few Class 47s on some of its services, but these, together with some of the HST sets, are now rapidly being replaced by the new Class 220 'Voyager' trains. With the introduction of these new units, loco-hauled passenger services through the Thames and Chiltern area have become a rarity as elsewhere on the network.

Freight services in the Thames and Chiltern area are operated by EWS using Classes 37, 56, 58, 59, 60 and 66 with the latter class of locomotives now being predominant on most services. Royal Mail trains are operated with the new Class 67s, and Freightliner services still produce Class 47s, but also Class 57s and, increasingly, Class 66s.

Although the international freight terminal at Morris Cowley has closed, on 20 November 2001 a new car train service, conveying the new Mini to Europe, was inaugurated by BMW with Class 60 No 60085, named *MINI Pride of Oxford*, hauling the first train out of the new railhead at Cowley.

First Great Western HSTs and Heathrow Express EMUs are serviced at Old Oak Common, where a servicing depot is being built for the new Class 180 units. The locomotive depot and works are now an important repair and servicing depot for EWS locomotives. Thames Trains Class 165 and 166 units are serviced at Reading. EWS freight locomotives are also stabled at Acton and Didcot, where a small works and refuelling bay has been constructed.

For the steam enthusiast, the Chinnor & Princes Risborough Railway has gone from strength to strength and is now looking to extend its line through to Princes Risborough. The Cholsey & Wallingford Railway is currently operating with diesel traction, but sees the occasional visiting steam engine. At Didcot Railway Centre the Great Western Society has at last obtained the 'centre sidings' and is looking to extend visitor facilities. The new land will expand the site from its present 16 acres to about 20 acres.

Acton

The 5.5pm service from Paddington to Weston-super-Mare, hauled by 'King' class 4-6-0 No 6012 *King Edward VI* speeds through Acton Main Line on 8 August 1959. This station was opened by the Great Western on 1 February 1868 and was enlarged from two to four platforms with the construction of new relief lines in September 1877.

A First Great Western HST passes on Sunday, 9 September 2001 with the 10.30 service from Paddington to Weston-super-Mare. Today, facilities have been reduced to the minimum, with a couple of shelters provided for customers. The down main platform was removed some years ago. The new station entrance and ticket office can be seen on the centre road bridge, and the overhead electric wires are for the Heathrow Express service which was introduced on 23 June 1998. *GW Trust/Author*

Westbourne Park

The station building at Westbourne Park is seen here on 30 January 1923. The entrance to the Great Western station is in the distance and the entrance for the Metropolitan electrified line to Hammersmith is on the left. The ex-Great Western station was closed on 2 December 1991, after which it was completely removed to allow for track remodelling.

On 15 July 2001, the entrance building is still very much intact, although the lettering on the pediments has been removed. *GW Trust/Author*

Ealing Broadway

The attractive station entrance at Ealing Broadway was constructed by the Great Western in circa 1877. The entrance building stood on the road overbridge and is pictured here on 14 July 1947.

As can be seen, it has since been demolished and replaced by the concrete structure shown here in this 12 April 2001 view. One has to ask what the planners were thinking of when they allowed such an attractive building to be removed. *GW Trust/Author*

Ealing Broadway

Great Western 'Star' class 4-6-0 No 4012 *Knight of the Thistle* passes through Ealing Broadway in April 1947 with an up Bristol service. On the right is the London Underground station for the District and Central lines.

On 12 April 2001, Class 165 DMU No 165109 runs through with a service from Bedwyn. Apart from some refurbishment the general layout of the station itself remains largely unchanged.
GW Trust/Author

Wharncliffe Viaduct

A Great Western 'Castle' class 4-6-0 on a down service crosses Wharncliffe Viaduct on 10 October 1934. The viaduct was named after Lord Wharncliffe, an early supporter of the Great Western. It was completed in August 1837 and comprises eight 70ft span arches which carry the line over the Brent Valley.

It is difficult to get the same angle today, due to a 1930s housing estate and a great deal of undergrowth. Class 66 No 66073 crosses the viaduct with a stone train for Acton Yard on 12 April 2001. *GW Trust/Author*

Colnbrook

The main intermediate station on the Staines branch was at Colnbrook. This picture, taken around the end of the 19th century, shows the station building, the signalbox, and the level crossing over the old Bath Road. A family wait at the crossing as a Great Western 'Metro' 2-4-0T passes by.

After closure this part of the branch served a fuel oil terminal for nearby Heathrow.

West Drayton & Yiewsley

West Drayton & Yiewsley was the junction station for the Uxbridge Vine Street and Staines branches. The main line platforms are seen here on 21 June 1958 as 'Castle' class 4-6-0 No 7023 *Penrice Castle* speeds through with the 3.45pm service from Paddington to Fishguard Harbour.

Although the platform awnings have been removed, the original buildings have been retained. The up and down main platforms are now for emergency use only. On 15 July 2001, a First Great Western HST passes with a Paddington to Swansea service. Notice the up relief platform, left, retains its platform awning. *GW Trust/Author*

Today, although the track is still in situ, the rail link to the fuel depot is closed. The station site is almost directly under the flight path into Heathrow Airport and on 6 May 2001 a Boeing 737 passes overhead; planes were coming in every couple of minutes. The crossing is now fenced off, but the old station house remains relatively intact. The signalbox was closed on 19 March 1967. *GW Trust/Author*

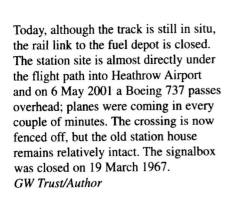

Staines West

Ex-Great Western diesel railcar No W30W stands at Staines West on 21 June 1958 with the 3.40pm service to West Drayton. Staines West was opened on 2 November 1885, the station being converted from a private house. Passenger services over the branch were withdrawn on 27 March 1965.

The building, which is listed, has seen a number of uses over the years, but has in recent months been tastefully converted into luxury flats. The old goods yard (behind the photographer) is now covered with a new housing estate. This was the scene on 6 May 2001, showing the recently converted building; its railway origins are maintained by the buffer stops and the Staines West sign on the car park retaining wall.
GW Trust/Author

Uxbridge Vine Street

'9400' class 0-6-0PT No 9409 stands at Uxbridge Vine Street after arriving with the 1.27pm service from Paddington on 21 June 1958. After closure to passengers, the station continued to be used for goods traffic until this was withdrawn on 24 February 1964.

Cowley

The second branch from West Drayton ran to Uxbridge Vine Street. This single-line branch was opened by the Great Western on 8 September 1856. Cowley (Middlesex) was the only intermediate station on the branch and was opened on 2 October 1904 when the line was doubled. It is pictured here on 8 August 1959 with diesel railcar No W21W operating the shuttle service to and from Uxbridge.

Passenger services were withdrawn on 8 September 1962, and goods services on 24 February 1964. Today, only the cutting remains although some of the station fencing is still in situ. The bridge has been removed and the cutting filled in and a roundabout now marks the spot where the bridge once stood.
A. Delicata/Author

For many years after closure, the site of Vine Street was used as a car park, but as can be seen in this picture taken on 25 November 2001, it has now been covered with a new office block.
GW Trust/Author

Slough

A down empty stock train hauled by ex-Great Western '4300' class 2-6-0 No 7302 passes through Slough on 22 September 1956. The station pictured here was constructed during 1886, and replaced the old Brunel-designed single-sided station which was opened by the GWR on 4 June 1841.

On 15 July 2001, the customary HST speeds through on a service to South Wales, while Class 165 No 165002 waits in the down bay with a service to Windsor. Apart from some upgrading the station shows little change, although the west end bay had been removed in October 1961. *GW Trust/Author*

Slough Shed

Slough engine shed stood west of the station and alongside the Windsor branch and is seen here in the late 1940s with an assortment of Great Western 2-6-2Ts and 0-6-0PTs. The shed supplied engines for local suburban services including the Windsor branch and the old Wycombe Railway branch from Maidenhead to Aylesbury. Opened by the GWR in 1868 the shed building was, over the years, enlarged and modernised, with a new roof being constructed during 1952. It was closed to steam in June 1964.

The site is now the station car park and was photographed on 15 July 2001.
GW Trust/Author

Windsor

The Slough to Windsor branch was opened on 8 October 1849. The original station at Windsor was constructed of wood, but between 1895 and 1897, it was replaced by a fine brick and stone building. A new 'Royal' side to the station containing an overall roof was constructed by the Great Western as a Diamond Anniversary gift to Queen Victoria. The public entrance to the new station is pictured here, probably soon after opening.

In recent years, much of the station has been converted into a tourist arcade and when I visited the station on 12 April 2001 the main entrance hall housed a craft fair. *GW Trust/Author*

Windsor

Diesel railcar No W30W stands at Windsor, Platform 1 on 12 June 1956 with the 4.54pm service to Slough. At this time, four platforms were in use, but during 1968/9 Platforms 2, 3 and 4 were taken out of use, and during December 1981, Platform 1 was shortened.

On 12 April 2001, Class 165 No 165004 waits at Windsor & Eton Central with the Slough shuttle service. The 'Royal' side of the station can be seen on the right. *GW Trust/Author*

Maidenhead

The 12.33pm stopping service from Paddington to Reading, hauled by ex-Great Western 'Modified Hall' 4-6-0 No 6973 *Bricklehampton Hall*, departs from Maidenhead on 16 February 1958.

Class 165 No 165126 arrives at Maidenhead on 12 April 2001 with a Paddington-Reading service. Apart from the motive power and the removal of the waiting room chimney, the station shows little change. *B. W. Leslie/Author*

Shiplake

A turn-of-the-century view of Shiplake on the Twyford to Henley branch with '517' class 0-4-2T No 463 waiting to depart with a Henley train. A single-platform station was opened here on 1 June 1856, but was replaced with a new island platform during 1898 when the branch was doubled.

Maidenhead

Maidenhead was the junction station for the Wycombe Railway branch to Bourne End, High Wycombe, Princes Risborough and Aylesbury. Pictured here in c1911 is a 'Metro' class 2-4-0T standing at Platform 5 with a service from High Wycombe . In the up relief platform is a Thames Valley stopping service. The low level entrance to the station can be seen on the right. The extended platform awnings date from the 1930s.

Today, the old Wycombe branch terminates at Bourne End with services reversing and running through to Marlow. On 12 April 2001 a two-car Class 165 unit waits at the branch platform with a service to Marlow while No 165109 arrives at the main platform with a Thames Trains stopping service. *GW Trust/Author*

The Henley branch was singled during June 1961 and Shiplake remained a passing point until the down platform line was taken out of use in May 1969. All trains today use the old up platform and a car park encroaches on what was once the down line. Notice the original station running-in board displayed at the end of the car park. *GW Trust/Author*

Reading

This undated view shows the imposing station entrance at Reading. Opened on 30 May 1868, the building was constructed using brick and bath stone, replacing an earlier wooden structure. On the right is the South Eastern Railway station. The statue of King Edward VII was presented to the town by Martin Sutton, founder of Suttons Seeds.

The entrance to the station is now via the Brunel Arcade (right), which was built over the site of the old South Eastern station. The old entrance building has been restored and converted to the Three Guineas bar and restaurant. King Edward VII's statue has been moved into the centre of a new roundabout. *GW Trust/Author*

Reading Caversham Goods

The lower goods yard at Reading Vastern Road in 1904, with Caversham Road signal works on the extreme left. The signal works, which had been established on the site in 1859, was closed on 29 June 1984. During the 1960s many of the sidings at Vastern Road were removed, and the yard was finally closed in 1987.

The site is now covered by industrial development and this picture was taken from the station car park on 24 February 2001. In the foreground is the large Post Office depot; other buildings are currently occupied by Courts Furniture and Toys R Us. *GW Trust/Author*

Reading Central Goods (Coley)

An 'overflow' goods yard was constructed at Reading, adjacent to the Kennet & Avon Canal at Coley. Opened on 4 May 1908, it was known as Reading Central Goods. The yard is pictured here in 1919.

Reading Central Goods was closed on 25 July 1983, and in recent years a new relief road has been constructed through the site. Taken from the same road bridge, the row of cottages on the right provides a reference point for both pictures. *GW Trust/Author*

Mortimer

Mortimer is the first station south of Reading on the Basingstoke branch and is pictured here around the turn of the last century. The station was opened on 1 November 1848, and access to the down platform at this time was via the road bridge. The goods shed was closed on 17 June 1963 and the signalbox on 28 June 1966.

During the 1990s, the station was refurbished with a new footbridge; however, the main station building remains pretty much intact. On 24 February 2001, Class 165 No 165123 calls with a Thames Trains service from Basingstoke to Reading.
GW Trust/Author

Thatcham

An up service to Paddington comprising the 2.15pm ex-Minehead and 12.35pm ex-Ilfracombe, hauled by 'King' class 4-6-0 No 6021 *King Richard II*, speeds through Thatcham on 30 July 1960.

Basingstoke

The terminus of the branch was Basingstoke where the Great Western connected with the London & South Western lines. The terminus station is seen here in the 1920s, with the LSWR station on the left. Basingstoke GWR was closed to passengers on 1 January 1932.

Local services from Reading now use the bay platform at Basingstoke. Part of the old station site is covered by a car park and a South West Trains training centre so it is difficult to get the same angle. In this picture, taken on 28 October 2001, the Great Western Hotel provides the reference point.
GW Trust/Author

Thatcham is now served by Thames Trains services between Paddington and Bedwyn. The station has been extensively refurbished, and the old buildings have been replaced by modern structures as seen on 4 February 2001.
GW Trust/Author

Newbury

The down 'Cornish Riviera Express', the 10.30am service from Paddington to Penzance, hauled by 'King' class 4-6-0 No 6028 *King George VI* storms through Newbury on 30 July 1949. The station was the junction for branch services to Lambourn, Didcot and Southampton.

Today, almost all First Great Western services to the West are operated using HSTs. On 4 February 2001 the 10.15am service from Penzance passes Newbury en route to Paddington. The passenger footbridge alongside the road bridge has now been removed. *GW Trust/Author*

Welford Park

Ex-GWR '5700' class 0-6-0PT No 3738, now preserved at the Didcot Railway Centre, stands at Welford Park with the 10.15am service from Newbury to Lambourn on 14 March 1959. The unusual low level signalbox was opened on 7 February 1909 and was closed on 3 July 1962. The branch closed to passengers on 4 January 1960, but remained open for goods traffic until 30 June 1973 to serve the Air Ministry sidings at Welford Park.

Speen

The 12¼-mile long Lambourn Valley Railway, which ran from Newbury to Lambourn, high up on the Berkshire downs, was opened on 4 April 1898. In this picture the branch service from Newbury, hauled by Great Western '850' class 0-6-0ST No 2007, pauses at Speen en route to Lambourn in January 1936. The station was closed on 4 January 1960.

There is no trace of the station today, but the service road leading to 'The Sydings' follows the approximate line of the trackbed; 4 February 2001.
GW Trust/Author

Visiting the site on 4 February 2001 in heavy rain meant the whole area was a quagmire, but as can just be seen, both platforms remain in situ. The booking office from this station is also now preserved at the Didcot Railway Centre.
GW Trust/Author

Lambourn

Great Western diesel railcars saw regular use over the Lambourn branch. Standing at the terminus is car No W18W prior to its run back to Newbury. The station seen here was constructed by the Great Western in 1910 and replaced the original wooden structure. The section between Lambourn and Welford Park was closed completely on 4 January 1960.

For a number of years after closure, the site was in industrial use, but in recent years has been covered by new housing. The access road marks the site of the platform; 4 February 2001. *Hugh Ballantyne/Author*

Compton

Ex-Great Western 'City' class 4-4-0 No 3440 *City of Truro* stands at Compton on 13 July 1957 with a service from Didcot. Originally built as a single line, this northern stretch of the DN&S was doubled during 1943, the concrete footbridge and down platform being a World War 2 addition. After closure to passengers in September 1962, the station building was used as a goods office, but on 10 August 1964 goods traffic was withdrawn from Compton and the building was sold for use as a private residence.

Upton & Blewbury

The northern section of the Didcot, Newbury & Southampton Railway was opened on 13 April 1882 and ran from Didcot East Junction to Newbury, the southern section running from Newbury to Shawford Junction, where it connected with the LSWR line to Southampton. This section was opened some years later, on 1 January 1901. Originally constructed as a single line, it was doubled during World War 2, using Italian prisoner of war labour. Upton & Blewbury was the first station south of Didcot on the DN&S and is seen here with 'Duke' class 4-4-0 No 3272 *Fowey* on a service from Didcot to Southampton. The picture was taken sometime between 1925 and 1930 when the engine was allocated to Didcot.

The station was closed on 10 September 1962. Today it is in use as a private residence, and can just be seen through the trees on 4 February 2001. *GW Trust/Author*

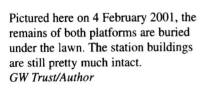

Pictured here on 4 February 2001, the remains of both platforms are buried under the lawn. The station buildings are still pretty much intact. *GW Trust/Author*

Burghclere

South of Newbury the southern section was doubled in 1942. On 14 March 1959, ex-GWR '2251' class 0-6-0 No 3206 arrives at Burghclere with the 12.25pm service from Newbury to Eastleigh. This station was closed to passengers on 7 March 1960.

Today, the station building has been tastefully restored and extended. The owners have even placed a couple of Great Western signs on the walls. The shell of the wartime brick signalbox is also still in situ, in the yard just south of the station; 4 February 2001. *GW Trust/Author*

Winchester Chesil

'City' class 4-4-0 No 3440 *City of Truro* stands at Winchester Chesil on 13 July 1957, with a Southampton to Didcot service. *City of Truro* had been taken out of retirement at York Railway Museum to work enthusiasts' specials and was 'earning its keep' so to speak, working stopping services over the DN&S line.

Highclere

Highclere station, looking south, depicted here in 1921. This was one of the passing points on the original single line, south of Newbury.

The absence of leaves on the trees allows a view of the platform edge and waterlogged trackbed on 14 February 2001. The station building, as with a number of others on the route, is now a private dwelling. *GW Trust/Author*

Winchester Chesil was closed to passengers on 7 March 1960 and today the site contains a multi-storey car park. Although the tunnel remains, notice the way the ground has been built up from railway days. A replica of the station building has been constructed and can be seen at the 'Milestones' museum at Basingstoke. *GW Trust/Author*

Hungerford

'King' class 4-6-0 No 6002 *King William IV* passes through Hungerford in August 1961 with a down West of England service.

On a wet 4 February 2001, a Thames Trains service, with Class 165 No 165109, from Paddington to Bedwyn pulls into Hungerford. The down yard, which was closed in 1971, is now a car park and also contains some industrial units. Note that the up platform has been extended. *GW Trust/Author*

West Ruislip

The 'new' line from Old Oak West Junction to Aynho Junction was opened in stages between 1903 and 1910 and provided the Great Western with a shorter route to Birmingham. West Ruislip was opened on 2 January 1906, and is seen here from the footbridge as 'Castle' class 4-6-0 No 7036 *Taunton Castle* passes by with a down service to Birmingham and Wolverhampton. The chalked reporting number is from an earlier working. On the left are the depot and sidings of the Central Line which terminates here.

The windows on the footbridge are now sealed so the same view is not possible. The station has been refurbished and the down platform widened over what was the down relief line. Class 168 No 168109 passes on 12 April 2001 with an up Chiltern Trains service from Birmingham Snow Hill to Marylebone.
Peter Stears/Author

Beaconsfield

Beaconsfield was opened on 2 March 1906 and is seen here in 1912 as a Great Western 'Bulldog' class 4-4-0 arrives with an up stopping service to Paddington.

The up and down through lines were removed in December 1975 and the station has since been refurbished by Chiltern Railways as seen here on 15 July 2001. Class 165 No 165027 arrives with the 08.50 service from Bicester North to Marylebone. *GW Trust/Author*

High Wycombe

Looking down at the station entrance at High Wycombe in May 1901. Many inhabitants have turned out to welcome members of the Buckinghamshire Yeomanry on their return from duty in South Africa. The station was rebuilt during 1905/6 when the route was upgraded by the Great Western & Great Central Joint Committee.

In recent years, Chiltern Railways has refurbished the station, with new ticket barriers and a second ticket office being introduced in 1999. The footbridge has long gone and passengers now reach the staggered up platform via a subway. The forecourt is now used for taxis and short-term parking. Notice also the ornate lamp post in this view of 25 February 2001. *GW Trust/Author*

Loudwater

Up and down services pass at Loudwater on the ex-Wycombe Railway branch from Maidenhead to High Wycombe. The branch was opened by the Wycombe Railway on 1 August 1854; it was extended through to Thame on 1 August 1862, and to Kennington Junction, south of Oxford, on 24 October 1864. Loudwater was situated just south of High Wycombe, and is seen here on 21 June 1958 as ex-Great Western '6100' class 2-6-2 No 6122 on the 12.25pm service from High Wycombe to Maidenhead passes fellow class member No 6115 on the 12.11pm service from Maidenhead to High Wycombe. Passenger services were withdrawn between High Wycombe and Bourne End on 4 May 1970.

The station area is now covered by a small industrial estate and is pictured here on 25 February 2001.
GW Trust/Author

Princes Risborough

The north end of Princes Risborough pictured here in 1957. Speeding through on the down main line is 'Modified Hall' class 4-6-0 No 6960 *Raveningham Hall* with a down fast service. Standing in the down platform is '5700' class 0-6-0PT No 5755 on a service to Watlington, and in the down bay is diesel railcar No W16W on a service to Oxford.

The refurbished station is seen here on 2 January 2001; one hopes it will not be long before the Chinnor & Princes Risborough trains use the down bay again. *N. C. Simmons/Author*

Princes Risborough

The 2.25pm service from Aylesbury to High Wycombe departs from Princes Risborough on 10 June 1962 hauled by ex-Great Western '1400' class 0-4-2T No 1455. The downgrading of the cut-off route during the late 1960s saw the down platform closed and the footbridge removed. However, during 1999, the down platform was reopened and a new footbridge constructed, complete with lifts for the disabled. The Chinnor & Princes Risborough Railway hopes to run its trains into what would be Platform 4.

The rebuilt down platform and footbridge can be seen here on 2 January 2001 as Class 168 No 168113 arrives with a service from Marylebone to Warwick Parkway. *L. Sandler/Author*

Little Kimble

The 10.35am auto-train service from Aylesbury to Princes Risborough calls at Little Kimble on 3 June 1962, hauled by '1400' class 0-4-2T No 1455. The 7½-mile branch from Princes Risborough to Aylesbury was opened by the Wycombe Railway on 1 October 1863.

The station is now an unstaffed halt and is seen here on 2 January 2001 as Class 165 No 165028 departs with the 10.17 Chiltern Railways service from London Marylebone to Aylesbury. The station building is now in private use.
L. Sandler/Author

Chinnor

The Watlington branch was opened by the Watlington & Princes Risborough Railway on 15 August 1872. One of the intermediate stations was Chinnor, seen here in 1957. The branch was closed to passengers on 1 July 1957 and the station demolished.

Aylesbury

The Great Western & Great Central and Metropolitan & Great Central Joint station at Aylesbury. Aylesbury was the terminus for former Wycombe Railway services from Princes Risborough, the original station here being opened on 1 October 1863. However, a new station, as seen here in the 1930s, was opened in March 1899 by the GW&GC and Met & GC companies.

Seen from the same footbridge on 2 January 2001, Class 165 No 165023 prepares to depart with the 11.08 service to Marylebone. The station is now operated by Chiltern Railways, and although retaining many of its original features, has been extensively refurbished. *GW Trust/Author*

The section from Princes Risborough to Chinnor is now operated by the Chinnor & Princes Risborough Railway, with Chinnor the headquarters of the railway. In recent years a new station has been completely built by the volunteers, and is seen here in January 2001. One word comes to mind: superb! What a credit to the railway society.
J. D. Edwards/Author

Watlington

The terminus station at Watlington, seen here shortly after closure in July 1957. The original intention was to link the line to the Wallingford branch but lack of finances soon scuppered this idea.

The remains of the station are on private land, but any chance of the preserved railway reaching Watlington is just a pipe dream as the trackbed has now been split west of Bledlow by the M40 motorway. This is sad as the station still survives, just, and can be seen behind the undergrowth on 2 January 2001. On the right, the old carriage shed is used for storing farm machinery. *J. D. Edwards/Author*

Haddenham

The down platform at Haddenham seen here on 23 September 1956. The station stood on the Paddington to Wolverhampton direct line and was opened on 1 July 1910. The rundown of services over the route saw the station close on 7 January 1963. The signalbox, however, lasted a little longer, closing on 18 April 1966. The line was singled between Princes Risborough and Bicester during October 1968.

The remains of the down platform can be seen in this view taken on 2 January 2001. During the 1980s, services over the Chiltern line were operated by Network SouthEast, and on 3 October 1987 it opened a new station, Haddenham & Thame Parkway, just to the north of the old station. In 1998, due to an increase in traffic, Chiltern Railways, who now operate the services, doubled the single-line section between Princes Risborough and Bicester. At the same time, a new platform and footbridge were installed at Haddenham.

The 'new' station is seen here on 2 January 2001; on the left, Class 168 No 168003 departs with the late-running 10.15 service from High Wycombe to Birmingham, while on the right, No 168110 arrives with the 09.30 service from Warwick Parkway to Marylebone. *J. S. Gilks/Author*

Cholsey

A view of Cholsey taken on 4 May 1957 as 'Hall' class 4-6-0 No 4903 *Astley Hall* speeds through with a service from Oxford to Paddington. Cholsey & Moulsford was opened on 29 February 1892 and replaced an earlier station that stood about a mile further east. The signalbox on the up main platform, partially seen behind the 'Hall', was closed on 9 August 1965.

On 1 September 2001, an up HST rushes past with an up service from Bristol. The main line platforms, although still in situ, are not in public use. *GW Trust/Author*

Cholsey

'1400' class 0-4-2T No 1441 stands in the bay at Cholsey on 21 June 1958 after arriving with the 5.55pm service from Wallingford. The branch was opened on 2 July 1866, passenger services over the 3½-mile line were withdrawn on 15 June 1959, and goods services on 13 September 1965. After that date, the station land at Wallingford was sold for housing and the shortened branch was operated as a long siding serving the ABM malt plant.

Today, what is left of the branch is operated by the Cholsey & Wallingford Railway. On 1 September 2001 the branch train, seen here in the bay at Cholsey, was hauled by ex-BR Class 08 diesel shunter No 08123 with fellow class members (and one-time Guinness brewery locos) Nos 08022 and 08060 on the other end — three coaches and three '08's — an interesting combination!
GW Trust/Author

43

Didcot

'Castle' class 4-6-0 No 5084 *Reading Abbey* speeds through Didcot on 4 May 1957 with the 4.55am service from Fishguard Harbour to Paddington. The station was rebuilt in 1886, and in recent years, many of the platform buildings have been removed or replaced.

A First Great Western HST arrives on 21 October 2001 with a service from Bristol to Paddington. In the sidings on the right are Class 37 No 37707 and Class 60 No 60004. *GW Trust/Author*

Uffington

Uffington was opened on 1 June 1864 and was the junction station for the branch to Faringdon. The station is seen here on 24 August 1958 as ex-Great Western '5600' class 0-6-2T No 5697 prepares to run up the branch to collect the goods for Didcot Yard. The signalbox, which was opened in 1897, was closed on 3 March 1968. Uffington was closed to passengers on 7 December 1964.

Didcot Transfer Shed

The old Great Western broad gauge-standard gauge transfer shed at Didcot. Erected circa 1863, the shed stood alongside the Great Western main line, and adjacent to the old horse provender store.

In 1979, the shed was dismantled by members of the Great Western Society and re-erected at the railway centre. Today, a slightly shortened shed is used as Burlescombe station on the branch demonstration line. The original site of the shed is now covered by the Parkway station car park. *GW Trust/Author*

The site of the station is now partially covered by a signal relay building. The large girder bridge seen in the first picture, which was installed in 1897 to replace a level crossing, has in recent years been replaced by a new concrete road bridge. A First Great Western HST passes by on the main line with a service from Bristol on 29 April 2001. *GW Trust/Author*

Appleford Crossing

Just north of Didcot is Appleford Crossing, seen here c1920. The road across the railway was no more than a track at this time, serving a local farm and later some gravel pits. This was the approximate site of the original station at Appleford, which was opened by the Oxford Railway in June 1844 and closed in 1849. The signalbox seen here was demolished in an accident on 25 September 1952 and subsequently rebuilt.

The replacement box was reduced to a ground frame in 1965, and is seen here on 29 April 2001. It still controls the crossing and also a siding into the nearby waste tip. The crossing gates have been replaced by barriers and a new road has been built, which also serves the nearby tip. *GW Trust/Author*

Faringdon

The 3½-mile Faringdon Railway opened on 1 June 1864 from Uffington to Faringdon, where the small but attractive stone station with its interesting twin-hipped roofs is seen in 1919. The branch closed to passengers on 31 December 1951, but remained open for goods traffic until 1 July 1963.

The second picture shows the station building on 24 August 1958, in use as a goods office.

The third view, taken on 24 March 2001 sees the building, which is now listed, currently in use as a country produce store. *GW Trust/Author*

Culham

'Hall' class 4-6-0 No 6910 *Gossington Hall* passes through Culham with a northbound goods service from Reading to Oxford Hinksey Yard on 30 January 1965. Opened on 12 June 1844 as Abingdon Road, it was renamed Culham with the opening of the Abingdon Railway in 1856. The small signalbox was closed on 12 February 1961.

On 10 April 2001 Class 165 No 165109 arrives at Culham with a Thames Trains stopping service from Reading. The up Brunel-designed building is listed, but unused. The new up platform seen here on the left was brought into use during September 1993. *K. Farmer/Author*

Tiddington

Tiddington station stood midway between Thame and Wheatley. The station was opened on 1 June 1866, its two sidings serving a cattle dock and wood yard. In this undated view, but probably c1962, '5600' class 0-6-2T No 6664 arrives with a branch service from Oxford to Princes Risborough. By this date the small signalbox, installed around 1907, had been reduced to a ground frame. Tiddington was closed to passengers on 6 January 1963.

Wheatley

A view of Wheatley station from the adjacent road overbridge on 4 February 1959. Wheatley had two platforms, and was one of the passing points for branch services. The station was closed to passengers on 6 January 1963 but the line remained open for goods traffic until 1 May 1967. In 1969, the cutting and road bridge were filled in.

The site of Wheatley station, as seen on 2 January 2001, is now covered by a 1990s housing development, with the access road on the line of the old trackbed. The only evidence of a railway here is the 'Railway' public house which is still open. *GW Trust/Author*

Looking from the same spot on 28 March 2001 shows the remains of a Council road depot which stood on the site for a number of years after closure. Some original Great Western fencing is still evident at what was the station entrance. *GW Trust/Author*

Thame

I have to say that one of my favourite stations in Oxfordshire was at Thame. The station, with its overall roof, signalbox and goods yard, is shown here in this turn-of-the-last-century picture. This section of the Wycombe Railway branch from Wycombe to Kennington Junction was opened on 1 August 1862. Thame was the main station and crossing point on the branch and was closed to passengers on 6 February 1963. The signalbox was opened in 1892 and closed on 17 November 1968.

The track has now gone but both platforms remain in this view taken on 2 January 2001. Proposals to reopen this end of the branch fell through with the opening of Thame & Haddenham Parkway. The goods yard is now a small industrial estate, and the field on the left has an even larger one. *GW Trust/Author*

Oxford

A view of the south end of Oxford station taken from the Becket Street goods yard on 15 August 1959 as 'Castle' class 4-6-0 No 5018 *St Mawes Castle* departs with a semi-fast service to London. Oxford Station South signal box was closed on 18 October 1973, but the signal gantry on the right is still in use.

During 1998, Becket Street yard was converted into the station car park and connected to the station via a new footbridge. The station at Oxford was rebuilt during 1990.

Bledlow

Bledlow was opened by the Wycombe Railway on 1 August 1862. The station is pictured here in around January 1962 as '6100' class 2-6-2T No 6111 arrives with a service from Princes Risborough to Oxford. Passenger services were withdrawn on 6 February 1963, but this section of the branch remained open for oil trains to the Thame terminal until September 1991. The small signalbox, which controlled the station sidings and crossing, was closed on 15 September 1965.

A view of Bledlow on 28 April 2001. The station house is now a private residence and has been extended. The trackbed to the east is now a cycleway. *GW Trust/Author*

Seen from the same spot on 12 April 2001, Class 165 No 165137 departs with the 08.41 Thames Trains service to Reading and crosses the Botley Road bridge on its journey south. The building on the left is the new youth hostel which was officially opened on 3 May 2001. *J. D. Edwards/Author*

Eynsham

A lovely view of 'Metro' class 2-4-0T No 3562 at Eynsham on 25 September 1948 with a service to Fairford. Eynsham was opened by the Witney Railway on 14 November 1861, originally a single-platform station, but a new down platform was added in August 1944. Eynsham closed to passengers on 18 June 1962, although the station and goods shed remained intact until about 1987.

The whole site has been taken over by Oxford Instruments, and the wartime concrete platform was dismantled by the Great Western Society in 1984 and is now in use at Didcot Railway Centre. *GW Trust/Author*

Fairford

Fairford was the terminus of the East Gloucestershire Railway from Witney. Opened on 15 January 1873, the station was situated nearly a mile from the village. Viewed from the road bridge in June 1960, '7400' class 0-6-0PT No 7412 departs with the 1.50pm service on its 25-mile journey to Oxford. The branch was closed to passengers on 18 June 1962, the section from Witney to Fairford being lifted during the autumn of 1964.

The removal of the railway has seen the road overbridge removed and the road levelled. Today, the site is part of an industrial estate and although the old stone station building survived for a number of years, it has recently been removed. *GW Trust/Author*

Aynho

Aynho for Deddington, pictured here in 1932, was opened by the Oxford & Rugby Railway on 2 September 1850. The Great Western cut-off route from Ashendon Junction, which opened in July 1910, joined the old Oxford and Rugby line via the flyover junction just north of the station.

Aynho was closed to passengers on 2 November 1964. The up building and platform were removed, but the down building was used for a number of years by the local coal merchant. It was sold in 1993 and today has been tastefully restored into an interesting, if somewhat noisy, private residence. *GW Trust/Author*

Section 2 - Somerset, Dorset, Wiltshire and Bristol

This area was once served by a large number of branch lines, but the widespread closures of the 1960s mean almost none is left. In Somerset, sections of the Frome to Radstock and Witham to Yatton branches are still used for stone traffic and there are also two preserved lines. The East Somerset Railway runs trains from Cranmore, and the West Somerset Railway operates between Bishops Lydeard and Minehead, which at 20 miles, is Britain's longest preserved line.

The Great Western foothold in Dorset was once centred around the Yeovil to Weymouth line. This line was singled in 1968 but still provides an important cross-country route to the south coast. There were only two other Great Western branches in Dorset, both of which are now closed. The Weymouth to Abbotsbury branch closed on 1 December 1952 and the Maiden Newton to Bridport branch on 5 May 1975.

Wiltshire was well served by the Great Western, with branches to Calne, Highworth, Malmesbury and Devizes, all alas now closed. The Midland & South Western Junction Railway also bisected the county with its route from Cheltenham to Andover. The one-time headquarters of this railway was at Swindon Old Town and a short section of this route from Blunsdon is now operated by the Swindon & Cricklade Railway.

Swindon was at one time the most important engineering centre on the Great Western, but since the end of steam traction in 1965 and the subsequent rundown and closure of the works in 1986, the town has lost its railway status. However, Swindon's railway heritage has been preserved with the opening, during 2000, of 'Steam', a new railway museum which is situated in one of the old Great Western workshops.

Bristol Temple Meads is the second largest station on the former Great Western system and is still an important interchange station. The ex-Bristol & Exeter Railway locomotive depot at Bath Road closed in June 1995, with servicing switched to the smaller depot at Bristol Barton Hill, but HSTs continue to be serviced at St Philips

Marsh. During 2001, track was reinstated, for freight use, over part of the Portishead branch and extended on a new formation to Royal Portbury Dock, with services starting on 7 January 2002.

The line from Bathampton to Westbury and Salisbury is still an important through route connecting Southampton with Bristol and South Wales. The Thingley Junction to Trowbridge line was closed to passengers on 18 April 1966 but on 13 May 1985, a limited passenger service was introduced between Swindon and Melksham. This has now been supplemented with Wessex Trains services from Swindon to Southampton via Thingley Junction and Trowbridge. Wessex Trains is a new franchise which was inaugurated on 14 October 2001 and was formerly part of Wales & West.

Main line passengers services are operated by First Great Western and Virgin CrossCountry with HSTs. Secondary services are operated by Wessex Trains using Class 142, 143, 150, 153 and 158 DMUs. Freight services are operated by EWS using Classes 37, 56, 58, 60 and 66, and aggregate trains from the Mendip quarries are hauled by Mendip Rail Class 59s and EWS Class 66s.

Ogbourne

Ogbourne was situated on the Midland & South Western Junction line between Swindon and Marlborough. The station is seen here in this undated picture, as a Great Western 'Duke' class 4-4-0 passes through with a goods service to Marlborough. Ogbourne was closed on 11 September 1961.

The trackbed of the railway was used at this point for a new bypass. The old road, on the right, now enters the village under the new road instead of the railway. The entrance to the station was via the footpath on the left. Today, the remains of the trackbed end just behind the bus shelter. *GW Trust/Author*

Hannington

The 5½-mile Swindon & Highworth
Railway was opened from Highworth
Junction, east of Swindon, to Highworth
on 9 May 1883. Hannington was an
intermediate station on the branch and is
pictured here in the 1950s as ex-Great
Western '5800' class 0-4-2T No 5804
arrives with a Swindon to Highworth
service. The branch was closed to
passengers on 2 March 1953 but
remained open for goods traffic until
6 August 1962.

On 27 December 2000, the site was
being used by a farmer as a slurry
dump. The road bridge has been filled
in, but the remains of the platform can
still be seen. *R. H. G. Simpson/Author*

Swindon Works A' Shop

A view of the main erecting shop at Swindon on 18 March 1925. It was opened in 1900, and replaced the old broad gauge erecting shop. 'A' Shop, as it was known, was enlarged during 1921 to cover an area of 11½ acres.

With the rundown of the works, 'A' Shop was closed in 1986, and since then the site has been cleared. The whole area is now being redeveloped with car showrooms and housing, and on 14 August 2001, a new Persimmon Homes estate was under construction. *GW Trust/Author*

Wootton Bassett

Wootton Bassett was opened by the Great Western on 30 July 1841 and replaced a temporary station at Wootton Bassett Road. The station effectively became a junction with the opening of the Wootton Bassett to Patchway section of the South Wales main line on 1 May 1903. The station is seen here in September 1961 as 'Castle' class 4-6-0 No 5013 *Abergavenny Castle* passes by with the down 'South Wales Pullman', the 8.50am service from Paddington to Swansea High Street.

Swindon Works Weigh Shop

Adjacent to 'A' Shop was the locomotive Weigh Shop, pictured here in 1960. This is where locomotives were weighed and balanced. Standing outside, left, is 'Modified Hall' 4-6-0 No 6986 *Rydal Hall*.

Luckily, the Weigh Shop has survived, and today has been incorporated into Archers Brewery. *GW Trust/Author*

Wootton Bassett was closed to passengers on 4 January 1965. Seen from what was the up platform on 11 March 2001, a First Great Western HST speeds through with a down South Wales service. *GW Trust/Author*

Little Somerford

The up 'Red Dragon', the 7.30am service from Carmarthen to Paddington, hauled by 'King' class 4-6-0 No 6023 *King Edward II*, heads through Little Somerford station in June 1960. Little Somerford was opened on 1 May 1903 and closed to passengers on 3 April 1961.

On 27 June 2001, Class 60 No 60058 *John Howard* passes with an Avonmouth to Didcot coal train. The remains of the down platform can still be seen, but the whole of the old station area is now fenced off. *GW Trust/Author*

Chippenham

A view from the footbridge at Chippenham station on 24 March 1951 as 'Saint' class 4-6-0 No 2927 *Saint Patrick* enters the station with a service from Taunton to Paddington. *Saint Patrick* was withdrawn from service in December 1951.

On 31 March 2001, Class 165 No 165134 departs with the 09.09 First Great Western service from Oxford to Bristol. Rationalisation has seen Chippenham turned into an island platform with the up main platform closed. The tin shed on the right still survives, 50 years after the first view. *G. J. Jefferson/Author*

Malmesbury

The 6½-mile long Malmesbury Railway was opened on 18 December 1877. The branch originally left the Great Western main line at Dauntsey, but with the opening of the Badminton line it was diverted to the new station at Little Somerford. The terminus at Malmesbury is seen here on 30 August 1958 as '5800' class 0-4-2T No 5802 shunts the weekly goods service to Swindon.

The engine shed is listed and is seen here in use as a store on 11 March 2001. The rest of the station site is in industrial use. *GW Trust/Author*

Lacock Halt

'Hall' class 4-6-0 No 6943 *Farnley Hall* passes Lacock Halt on 6 November 1960 with the 10.10am service from Bristol to Weymouth. Lacock Halt was opened by the Great Western on 16 October 1905 and closed on 18 April 1966.

The line was singled in 1967 and has recently seen an increase in both passenger and freight traffic. The remains of the halt could still be seen on 31 March 2001. The nearby Lacock Abbey was the home of photography pioneer William Henry Fox Talbot. *GW Trust/Author*

Melksham

The 10.10am service from Bristol to Weymouth, diverted due to engineering works, passes through Melksham on 13 April 1960 hauled by 'County' class 4-6-0 No 1009 *County of Carmarthen*. Passenger services over the line were withdrawn on 18 April 1966, but it remained open for goods traffic until 13 May 1985 when passenger services were reinstated with a morning and evening service to and from Chippenham. This has now been supplemented with through South West Trains services between Swindon and Southampton.

Only part of the down platform is now in use and on 31 March 2001 the whole area was, in the author's opinion, quite frankly, a mess, however I understand that passenger facilities at Melksham are to be improved.
GW Trust/Author

Holt Junction

'Castle' class 4-6-0 No 7014 *Caerhays Castle* runs off the Devizes branch at Holt Junction in 1961 with a diverted West of England service. Holt Junction was closed to passengers on 18 April 1966, and the signalbox was closed on 26 February 1967.

On a foggy 22 October 2001 caravans cover part of the area. The station building survives and is used as an office for a local coal supply company. *GW Trust/Author*

Box

This terrific picture shows the small station at Box on 20 June 1959 as 'Castle' class 4-6-0 No 5085 *Evesham Abbey* works through with the 1.15pm service from Paddington to Bristol Temple Meads. The station, which was situated about half a mile west of Box Tunnel, was closed to passengers on 4 January 1965. The engine shed, which opened in 1845 and closed in 1919, was situated adjacent to the water tank, left.

There is little evidence of the old station now, and overgrown trees preclude the same angle, as a First Great Western HST on a Bristol to Paddington service climbs towards the tunnel on 16 April 2001. The road down to the station entrance was behind the trees on the right. *GW Trust/Author*

Bath Spa

'Castle' class 4-6-0 No 5098 *Clifford Castle* prepares to leave Bath Spa on 10 August 1963 with a Paddington to Bristol parcels service. This view was chosen as it shows to good effect the large signalbox above the down platform which was opened in September 1897 and closed on 21 January 1968.

The station has recently been refurbished, but the base of the old box can still be seen as a First Great Western HST pulls out with a service from Paddington to Bristol. Standing in the up platform is Class 158 No 158868 on a Cardiff to Weymouth service; 28 June 2001. *Hugh Ballantyne/Author*

Limpley Stoke

'5700' class 0-6-0PT No 9612 is depicted on the Camerton branch near the junction at Limpley Stoke in March 1958. The branch was closed for goods on 15 February 1951; however, the track was not recovered until September 1958.

On 26 June 2001, the Viaduct Hotel is obscured by trees, and the trackbed is now a service road leading to the warehouse of the Bath Furniture Mill. *GW Trust/Author*

Monkton Combe (Titfield)

Monkton Combe was an intermediate station on the Camerton branch from Limpley Stoke to Hallatrow. The branch was closed to passengers on 21 September 1925 and the section from Hallatrow to Camerton was lifted during 1932, thereby making Camerton the terminus of the branch. The section from Limpley Stoke to Camerton remained open for goods traffic until 15 February 1951. After closure the branch remained pretty much intact and during July 1952 was used for filming the Ealing comedy *The Titfield Thunderbolt*. Monkton Combe is seen here masquerading as Titfield on 26 July 1952.

This second view, taken on 19 April 1958, shows 0-6-0PT No 9612 at Monkton Combe on track recovery duty.

The same spot is seen on 28 June 2001 with garages built on the site of the old station. Notice however that the two gateposts at the station entrance still survive on each side of the second garage from the right. *GW Trust/Author*

Bristol Temple Meads

Another favourite location is the original Great Western terminus at Bristol Temple Meads. In this view, taken on 24 May 1958, '4575' class 2-6-2T No 5546 prepares to depart with the 11am service to Severn Beach. Also in view is Ivatt 2-6-2T No 41243.

On 14 August 2001, the only occupants are cars, for this part of the building is now a car park. Although the building has been restored, Brunel would probably turn in his grave at its use; what a mess. *GW Trust/Author*

Clifton Down

Clifton Down station opened on 1 October 1874 and was for a time the western terminus of the Clifton Extension Railway. On 1 September 1885, the line was opened for passenger traffic through Clifton Tunnel to Avonmouth, with Clifton Down becoming a through station. The station is pictured here in the 1930s, and shunting in the small yard is a Great Western 0-6-0PT. The station was reduced to an unstaffed halt on 17 July 1967.

Bristol Bath Road Shed

Great Western 'Bulldog' class 4-4-0 No 3433 moves off shed at Bristol Bath Road on 15 May 1936. The shed was built on the site of the old Bristol & Exeter depot and was opened by the GWR in December 1934. Bath Road was closed to steam in 1961 and converted to a diesel depot, which opened on 18 June 1962.

In June 1995, Bath Road was closed and facilities moved to Barton Hill. The buildings at Bath Road are empty and now devoid of tracks, as seen on 14 August 2001. *GW Trust/Author*

Seen from the same spot on 14 August 2001, the imposing stone entrance building is now a bar. The goods yard, which closed on 5 July 1965, has been covered by the Clifton Down shopping centre and private housing. *GW Trust/Author*

Avonmouth Dock

Avonmouth Dock station on 24 May 1958 with '6100' class 2-6-2T No 6137 on the 11.58am service from St Andrews Road to Bristol. On the left is the 11.35am Lawrence Hill to Severn Beach service hauled by BR Class 3 2-6-2T No 82037. Avonmouth Dock was opened on 1 September 1885. Originally only a single platform, the station was rebuilt and a new up platform added during 1926.

On 14 August 2001, Class 150 No 150254 waits to depart with a service to Bristol. The signalbox was closed on 19 January 1969 and although much has gone, the original brick-built station entrance on the down platform still survives (left). *GW Trust/Author*

Severn Beach

Severn Beach was an intermediate station on the branch from Chittening to Pilning Low Level, and was opened on 5 June 1922. The station is seen here on 24 May 1958. Standing at the through platform is the 2pm service to Bristol hauled by '4575' class 2-6-2T No 5559. Just arrived from Bristol is Swindon-built BR Standard Class 3 2-6-2T No 82039. The line in the foreground continued through to Pilning Low Level.

The line to Pilning closed on 23 November 1964. Today, only one platform is in use. and the station building has been replaced by a private house. On a sunny 14 August 2001 a couple wait at the station, not for a train but a connecting bus service to Avonmouth Dock station, as at the time of writing, a number of off-peak train services between Avonmouth and Severn Beach have been replaced by buses. *GW Trust/Author*

Pilning Low Level

A view of Pilning Low Level in the 1950s. This station was opened on 9 July 1928, with the low level branch connecting with the high level South Wales main line just beyond the level crossing. The section from Severn Beach to Pilning Low Level was closed on 23 November 1964.

The site has been cleared as seen on 14 August 2001. The only visible evidence of a railway here is part of the level crossing gate which still survives and can just be seen, left centre. The rest of the crossing is now in use at Didcot Railway Centre. *GW Trust/Author*

Pilning High Level

An up goods service hauled by a pair of ex-GWR 2-6-2Ts, with '5101' class No 5169 leading, climb up from Severn Tunnel and approach Pilning High Level on 17 June 1958. Pilning HL was opened on 1 December 1886 with the commencement of passenger services through the newly opened tunnel.

The station was deserted on 14 August 2001 apart from myself and a few local enthusiasts on the footbridge. Class 158 No 158822 passes with a Cardiff to Portsmouth service. The station is all but closed as the current timetable shows just one up and one down train a day stopping here. *GW Trust/Author*

Portishead

The 'new' terminus at Portishead on 27 August 1954 with diesel railcar No W28W on the 1.45pm service to Bristol Temple Meads. This station was opened on 4 January 1954 and replaced the previous one that was situated nearer the dock, which was closed on the same day.

Portishead was closed on 7 September 1964, and the site is now covered by a petrol station, as seen on 14 August 2001. During 2001 a section of the branch from Parsons Street Junction to the Royal Portbury Dock was reinstated for container traffic. *Hugh Ballantyne/ Author*

Brislington

The Saturdays-only 1.30pm service from Bristol to Frome arrives at Brislington hauled by '5700' class 0-6-0PT No 9668. This was the first station south of Bristol on the branch to Frome. It was closed to passengers on 2 November 1959.

The site is now derelict, and the concrete garage block is in a sorry state. However, the road bridge is still in situ and gives a reference point. The area behind the photographer is covered by a Tesco supermarket; 22 October 2001. *R. E. Toop/Author*

Pensford Viaduct

Pensford Viaduct on the Bristol to Frome line was opened on 3 September 1873 and is seen to good effect here on 14 March 1955 as ex-ROD 2-8-0 No 3032 passes with some coal empties to Radstock.

The viaduct is now a listed structure and is shown here on a wet and misty 22 October 2001. *Hugh Ballantyne/ Author*

Clutton

Clutton was an intermediate station on the Bristol to Frome branch. On 20 December 1958 '4500' class 2-6-2T No 4555 arrives with the 1.30pm service from Bristol to Frome. The low level goods yard can just be seen on the right. The station was closed to passengers on 2 November 1959, but the low level yard remained open for goods until closure on 10 June 1963.

The conifer trees mark the site of the station. Although the low level yard now contains a youth club and five-a-side football pitch, the base of the platform shelter on the left could still be seen on 14 April 2001. *GW Trust/Author*

Hallatrow

The 10.17am (SO) service from Bristol to Frome departs from Hallatrow on 31 October 1959 hauled by '5700' class 0-6-0PT No 9612.

Since closure, a large house has been built on the trackbed; part of the platform is still extant and has been landscaped into the garden. The original station building also survives (right) and has been incorporated into a house, as seen on 22 October 2001.
Hugh Ballantyne/Author

Farrington Gurney

Farrington Gurney was also situated on the branch from Bristol to Frome, and is seen here on 12 September 1959 as '5700' class 0-6-0PT No 8741 arrives with the 2.53pm service from Bristol. The station, or halt as it became, was closed on 2 November 1959.

Since then, the road bridge has been removed and the cutting filled. New houses occupy the area behind the wall. The main reference point is the 'Miners Arms', seen at the top left of both pictures. *GW Trust/Author*

Farrington Gurney

At Farrington Gurney, tickets were issued from the 'Miners Arms', and the ticket office can be seen at the bottom left. This close-up of the office was taken on 12 September 1959, the sign explaining that tickets can be purchased up until 7pm on weekdays by ringing the bell.

Today, the building has a new roof and is used as a store room for the pub. The present-day sign is obviously not original; 14 April 2001.
GW Trust/Author

Midsomer Norton & Welton

The Great Western station at Midsomer Norton & Welton, as '5700' class 0-6-0PT No 9668 arrives with the 1.30pm service from Bristol to Frome. The station was closed on 2 November 1959.

The site of the station is seen here on 22 October 2001. Part of the trackbed is a footpath and the rest has been fenced off. Station Road can be seen on the right. *R. E. Toop/Author*

Radstock West

On a bright summer's day, 4 July 1959, '5700' class 0-6-0PT No 5771 arrives at Radstock West with the 1.32pm service from Bristol to Frome. The signalman waits on the platform to take the single-line token. Radstock, at one time, boasted two stations, the Somerset & Dorset North station being a short distance away. Radstock West was closed to passengers on 2 November 1959, but remained open for coal traffic until 29 November 1965.

Today, one platform remains, and behind the graffiti-clad wall are houses. The building in the centre which was a tobacconists in 1959, is today a bicycle shop. One item that does survive is the signalbox which was removed in November 1975 and is now at Didcot Railway Centre (below right). In BR days, Radstock North box was renamed Radstock West, but at Didcot it has regained its original name; 14 April 2001. *GW Trust/Author*

Frome

A view of the station at Frome on 13 May 1952 with a new, Swindon-built BR Standard Class 3 2-6-2T, No 82000, on the 8.15am service to London Paddington. The coaches will be attached to the 8.38am up Paddington service at Westbury. The station, with its fine overall roof, was opened on 7 October 1850 and is now listed.

Frome is depicted here on 22 October 2001 without a train so as to show the restored building. *GW Trust/Author*

Frome

Today, Frome is served by Wessex Trains services between Bristol and Weymouth, but on 16 February 1958 'King' class 4-6-0 No 6025 *King Henry III* approaches Frome with the diverted 10.30am 'Cornish Riviera Express' from Paddington to Penzance.

On 13 March 2001, only one platform at Frome was in use. Radstock branch junction has gone and apart from diversions due to engineering work, main line services now bypass Frome. *GW Trust/Author*

Yatton

Yatton was the junction for the branch lines to Cheddar and Clevedon. The station was opened as Clevedon Road by the Bristol & Exeter Railway on 14 June 1841 and was renamed Yatton with the opening of the Clevedon branch on 28 July 1847. The Cheddar branch was opened 3 August 1869. On 24 May 1958 'Hall' class 4-6-0 No 4909 *Blakesley Hall* approaches Yatton with an up goods service from the West Country. The branch line to Clevedon can just be seen behind the locomotive.

Class 158 No 158827 enters Clevedon with an Exeter to Bristol service on 14 August 2001. The Cheddar branch platform is now a car park, and the Clevedon line is covered with housing. *GW Trust/Author*

Congresbury

An early postcard view of Congresbury on the branch to Cheddar. The station was initially opened with a single platform on 3 August 1869. However, with the opening of the Wrington Vale Light Railway in December 1901, Congresbury became a junction station and was provided with two platforms. The station closed to passengers on 9 September 1963.

Clevedon

The terminus at Clevedon, with '4575' class 2-6-2T No 4577 waiting to depart on 3 August 1953 with the 11am service to Yatton. As already mentioned, the 3½-mile branch from Yatton to Clevedon was opened on 28 July 1847. Goods services were withdrawn on 10 June 1963, and the branch was closed with the withdrawal of passenger services on 3 October 1966.

A Safeway supermarket and shopping arcade now cover the site of Clevedon station. The buildings on the left, and the church on the hill, are now the main reference points; 14 August 2001. *GW Trust/Author*

The whole area has now been covered by a new housing development. The road bridge has been removed and Station Close marks the site of the station; 14 August 2001. *GW Trust/Author*

Blagdon

Blagdon station was the terminus of the Wrington Vale Light Railway. The railway was supported by the Bristol Waterworks Company which built its reservoir at Blagdon. The light railway, which ran from Congresbury on the Yatton to Cheddar line to Blagdon, was opened on 4 December 1901. Passenger services did not last for long and were withdrawn on 14 September 1931. The line remained open for goods traffic but was closed completely on 1 November 1950. The station is seen here on 22 May 1929 with Great Western '517' class 0-4-2T No 540 on the 7.20pm branch passenger service to Yatton. After closure in 1950 the station lay derelict for a number of years, and is seen here on 2 August 1959.

The station has now been beautifully restored and forms part of a private residence. Nice touches include station lamps to light the drive, various GWR signs, and a restored guard's van body, as photographed on 16 April 2001.
GW Trust/Author

Draycott

Draycott station seen here on 15 July 1961 as ex-LMS 2-6-2T No 41202 arrives with the 10.30am service from Wells to Yatton. Draycott was closed on 9 September 1963.

A new house has now been built on the trackbed but the old station buildings, which can be seen on the left, are now in use as private dwellings; 14 April 2001. *GW Trust/Author*

Wookey

An Ivatt 2-6-2T arrives at Wookey with a service from Wells to Witham on 24 February 1962. Wookey was also closed on 9 September 1963.

The same angle is not possible today due to the large addition to the old goods shed. I have therefore included a view of the site of Wookey station from the road overbridge taken on 14 April 2001. *GW Trust/Author*

Cranmore

The 3.38pm service from Witham to Yatton arrives at Cranmore on 21 August 1958 behind '5700' class 0-6-0PT No 8744. Cranmore was opened on 9 November 1858. The line was closed to passengers on 9 September 1963, but remained open for goods traffic until 17 January 1966 although bitumen trains continued to run through to Cranmore from the main line at Witham until September 1985. The site was taken over by the new East Somerset Railway during 1971 and the first part was formally opened as a preserved line on 20 June 1975.

Shepton Mallet High Street

The Great Western station at Shepton Mallet High Street, pictured here in the early 1900s, was opened by the East Somerset Railway on 9 November 1858. On the left is Great Western '2721' class 0-6-0ST No 2729 on shunting duty, whilst arriving with a Witham to Yatton service is a '517' class 0-4-2T. No 2729 was converted to a pannier tank in September 1920 and withdrawn in March 1946.

Shepton Mallet was closed to passengers on 9 September 1963 and to goods traffic on 13 July 1964. The station building on the left still survives and is part of a small industrial estate which now covers the station area.
GW Trust/Author

When I visited the railway on 4 August 2001, the view was blocked by coaches, but only this platform now remains. I have expanded the view to show the station building which has been restored and extended, using materials from other railway buildings, including Lodge Hill station which was between Wookey and Cheddar. The platform canopy was rescued from Ash Vale station in Surrey.
Hugh Ballantyne/Author

Witham

Witham was the junction station for branch services to Shepton Mallet and Wells. The station was situated near the village of Witham Priory and was opened by the Wilts, Somerset & Weymouth Railway on 1 September 1850. The branch to Shepton Mallet was opened on 9 November 1858 and to Yatton on 5 April 1870. On 28 August 1960, 'King' class 4-6-0 No 6028 *King George VI* speeds through with an up service from Plymouth to Paddington. Witham was closed to passengers on 3 October 1966.

The site of the station is pictured here on 22 October 2001 as an HST passes with the 10.33 First Great Western service from Paddington to Plymouth. Witham East Somerset Junction to Cranmore and Merehead Quarry is on the right. A large signal relay building now stands on the site of the down platform. *GW Trust/Author*

Keinton Mandeville

The up relief 'Cornish Riviera Express', hauled by 'Castle' class 4-6-0 No 7006 *Lydford Castle* passes Keinton Mandeville on 19 September 1959. The station was closed on 10 September 1962.

Part of the down platform and also the small waiting room still survive, and on the up side the remains of the platform can still be entered by the original gate. The main station entrance is now covered by a garage and tyre depot as seen on 13 April 2001. *GW Trust/Author*

Wootton Rivers Halt

Wootton Rivers Halt stood on the West of England main line to the west of Savernake. It is seen here in September 1961 as the now-preserved 'Castle' class 4-6-0 No 5043 *Earl of Mount Edgcumbe*, passes with a down West of England express. The halt was opened on 24 September 1928 to serve the local community. One wonders how many passengers used it before it was closed on 18 April 1966.

The same scene on 16 April 2001; the site of the down platform can still be seen. *GW Trust/Author*

Patney & Chirton

Ex-Great Western '4700' class 2-8-0 No 4703 pounds through Patney & Chirton on 18 August 1956 with the 12.5pm service from Paddington to Plymouth. The '4700' class engines were regularly pressed into use on summer Saturday holiday trains to the South West.

Patney & Chirton was situated just west of Savernake and was the junction station for the Devizes line. It was closed to passengers on 18 April 1966 and the spot is now marked by the large footbridge, which is all that survives of the old station.
GW Trust/Author

Devizes

The branch from Patney entered Devizes via a 190yd-long tunnel, which is seen here on 30 August 1961. Leaving the tunnel is 'Castle' class 4-6-0 No 5034 *Corfe Castle* on the diverted 11.30am service from Paddington to Plymouth.

The tunnel entrance is at the end of a car park, seen here on 31 March 2001. It is currently used as a shooting range. *GW Trust/Author*

Devizes

Just beyond the tunnel was Devizes station, where on 16 November 1957, the 1.52pm service from Newbury to Westbury, hauled by 'Hall' class 4-6-0 No 5973 *Rolleston Hall*, waits to depart. The Devizes line was closed to passengers on 18 April 1966.

As can be seen, the station site is now covered by a car park. *GW Trust/Author*

Seend

Apart from Devizes, the main intermediate station on the branch was at Seend. The station is seen here in the early 1960s as 'Hall' class 4-6-0 No 4915 *Condover Hall* passes through with a diverted West of England service. The down platform loop was removed on 10 June 1956 and the station was closed on 18 April 1966.

The station yard is now used by a builders' merchants, but both platforms are still in situ behind the railway fence, which has been re-erected along the length of what was the down platform. *GW Trust/Author*

Lavington

Lavington was on the West of England main line west of Patney & Chirton. On 25 August 1956 the signalman watches as 'King' class 4-6-0 No 6024 *King Edward 1* passes with the down 'Cornish Riviera Limited', the 10.30am service from Paddington to Penzance. Lavington box was closed on 22 January 1979.

Little now remains of the station which closed on 18 April 1966 but part of the up platform can just be seen on the left. The station yard is now in industrial use. The 'King' has survived and operates many steam specials from its current base at Didcot Railway Centre. *GW Trust/Author*

Edington & Bratton

'Hall' class 4-6-0 No 5935 *Norton Hall* passes through Edington & Bratton with the 12.30pm service from Paddington to Weymouth on 12 March 1960. The station had been closed to passengers some years earlier, on 3 November 1952. The signalbox was closed on 22 February 1959.

The same scene on 13 April 2001. Nothing now remains of either platform and the yard is used by a dairy. However, the weighbridge building and the old goods shed still survive. *GW Trust/Author*

Salisbury Shed

The branch from Westbury to Salisbury was opened for passenger traffic on 30 June 1856. The Great Western engine shed at Salisbury is seen here in 1899, and part of the Great Western station is visible to the right of the picture. This shed was closed during the same year and was replaced by a new shed nearer the junction.

After closure, the site was used as a goods yard but in recent years has reverted to its former role with the construction of a South West Trains depot. The depot is pictured here on 27 June 2001. Part of the old Great Western station, which closed on 12 September 1932, is still visible behind the sidings on the right. *GW Trust/Author*

Sparkford

The 12.30pm service from Paddington to Weymouth hauled by 'Modified Hall' class 4-6-0 No 7924 *Thornycroft Hall* passes Sparkford on 19 September 1959. Sparkford was opened on 1 September 1860 and closed to passengers on 3 October 1966. The signalbox was closed on 30 November 1966.

The site of the station seen here on 4 August 2001. To take the picture I stood on the remains of the up platform. The line was singled on 12 May 1968, but is still quite busy. A new road bridge, carrying the A303, now bisects the view. *GW Trust/Author*

95

Hendford Halt

'4575' class 2-6-2T No 5521 pulls into Hendford Halt on 11 August 1939 with a service from Taunton to Yeovil Town. The large buildings behind the stone yard are part of the Westland aircraft factory. The halt was opened on 2 May 1932 and stood just to the west of a large brick-lined cutting and was closed on 15 June 1964.

On 14 April 2001, children play on the site of the halt. The stone yard is now part of a builders' merchants and is being redeveloped. The Westland factory can just be seen behind the trees.
GW Trust/Author

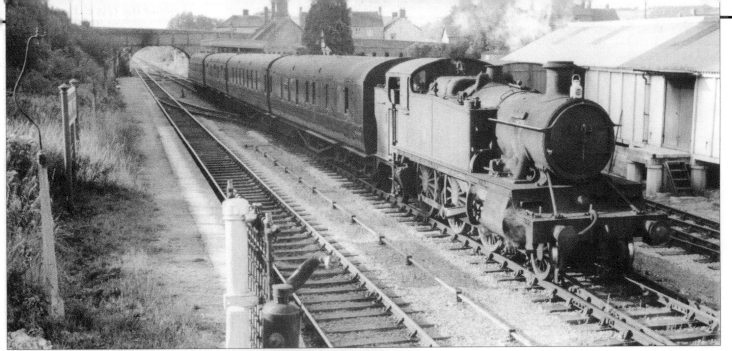

Langport West

The 10.5am service from Taunton to Yeovil arrives at Langport West in October 1961 hauled by '6100' class 2-6-2 No 6113. Passenger services were withdrawn on 15 June 1964.

As with many other closed station sites, Langport West is covered by an industrial estate and is seen here on 14 April 2001. The road overbridge gives the reference point.
GW Trust/Author

Abbotsbury

Diesel railcar No W24W stands at Abbotsbury station on 13 September 1952 with the 1.40pm service from Abbotsbury to Weymouth. The branch from Upwey Junction to Abbotsbury was opened on 9 November 1885.

Passenger services were withdrawn from the branch on 1 December 1952. Although the station lay derelict for many years, today it has been incorporated into a private house. As can be seen, the platform is still pretty much intact. The trackbed leads to the goods shed, which is still standing and is now in agricultural use; 14 April 2001. *GW Trust/Author*

Bridport

Bridport station is depicted here on 18 April 1958 as '4500' class 2-6-2T No 4562 arrives with the 1pm service to Maiden Newton. The 9¼-mile-long Bridport Railway was opened on 12 November 1857. The line was closed to goods on 5 April 1965 and to passengers on 5 May 1975.

Today, it is difficult to work out the exact position of the station as a large Co-operative supermarket and car park now cover the site; 14 April 2001. *GW Trust/Author*

Bridport West Bay

Bridport West Bay was the terminus of the branch from Maiden Newton to Bridport and is pictured here on 13 September 1952. The station was closed to passengers on 22 September 1930. Incredibly, it survived, and today has been restored as a tourist attraction.

The railway interest has been maintained with a couple of coaches and a signal. However, the illusion is somewhat destroyed by the large black boxes which are ladies' and gents' toilets; 14 April 2001. *GW Trust/Author*

Weymouth

An undated but probably pre-Grouping picture of the GWR station at Weymouth. The Great Western line from Dorchester Junction to Weymouth was opened on 20 January 1857. The station was also used by LSWR services from Waterloo, and in February 1958, the line to Weymouth became part of the Southern Region.

The old Great Western station is now gone and in its place is a much smaller, modern building. The terminus has been moved back to allow for extra car parking. The church on the right is almost the only surviving reference; 14 April 2001. *GW Trust/Author*

Weymouth Quay

The first picture (above right) was probably taken c1911-12, at which time a single line served the station at Weymouth Quay. The twin-funnelled ship is either the *Roebuck* or the *Reindeer*, both were built in 1897 by Vickers-Armstrong at Barrow and were operating on Channel Island services at this time. The horse-drawn postal vehicle on the left says 'GR' which dates the picture after 1910.

The second (right) view shows the *Saint Patrick*, and was taken in July 1939. Standing in the station, with a Channel Islands boat train, is Great Western '1366' class 0-6-0PT No 1371.The second platform at Weymouth Quay was constructed in 1932/3. *St Patrick* was launched on 15 January 1930, but was torpedoed and sunk whilst on war service in 1941.

Today (left), Channel Islands services are operated using fast trimaran boats, cutting journey times substantially. On 14 April 2001, *Condor Express* waits for its next load of passengers and cars. Although the tracks are still in situ. Weymouth Quay is no longer used by rail traffic. *GW Trust/Author*

Melcombe Regis

Melcombe Regis station stood on the LSWR & GWR Portland Harbour branch. Passenger services were withdrawn between Weymouth and Easton on 3 March 1952. Standing at the single platform on 13 September 1952 is diesel railcar No W24W with the 10.25am service from Abbotsbury to Weymouth. Note the row of wartime concrete machine gun posts on the platform.

The whole area has now been altered with the construction of a new ring road and, on 14 April 2001, the site of the station was being developed by McCarthy & Stone for retirement flats. *GW Trust/Author*

Easton (Portland)

'5700' class 0-6-0PT No 7782 stands at Easton on 15 December 1956 with a stone train for Portland and Weymouth. Easton was closed to passengers on 3 March 1952 but the line remained open for goods traffic until 5 April 1965.

Rodwell

Rodwell was an intermediate station on the Portland Railway, and is seen here on this undated picture taken from the high level road bridge. The station was closed on 3 March 1952.

Today, the trackbed has been turned into a footpath and cycleway.
GW Trust/Author

Seen from the same spot on 14 April 2001, retirement flats now occupy the station area and a gas pumping station is located on part of the old trackbed.
C. P. Boocock/Author

103

Creech St Michael

An undated but pre-1906 view of a Great Western 'Barnum' class 2-4-0 ploughing its way through the floods at Creech St Michael with an up stopping service. The line was quadrupled by the Great Western through here during 1931. Creech St Michael Halt was opened on 13 August 1928 and was closed on 5 October 1964.

Seen from the road overbridge at Creech St Michael on 15 April 2001, the 11.00 First Great Western HST service from Penzance to Paddington accelerates away on its journey to Paddington. Rationalisation saw the four-track layout reduced to two tracks in April 1986. *GW Trust/Author*

Lyng Halt

Lyng Halt was the only intermediate station on the Durston loop and is seen here on 16 May 1964. In this view the 12.37pm service from Yeovil to Taunton is hauled by '4575' class 2-6-2T No 4591. This line was part of the original route from Taunton to Yeovil and the section between Durston and Hendford was opened by the Bristol & Exeter Railway on 1 October 1853. Lyng Halt was opened on 24 September 1928 and closed on 15 June 1964.

Athelney

The branch from Durston connected with the Great Western main line at Athelney. The new cut-off route from Castle Cary to Cogload Junction was opened to passengers on 2 July 1906, and thereafter the short section of the old branch from here to Durston became known as the Durston loop. On 30 March 1957 '5400' class 0-6-0PT No 5411 waits to depart from Athelney with the 8.8am service from Castle Cary to Taunton. Athelney was closed to passengers on 15 June 1964.

On 1 September 2001, a First Great Western HST passes the site of Athelney station with the 11.06 'Atlantic Coast Express' service from Paddington to Newquay. *GW Trust/Peter Triggs*

Evidence of a railway can still be seen in this picture taken on 1 September 2001. *M. J. Fox/Peter Triggs*

Durston

Durston, pictured here in 1934, stood
on the main Bristol to Exeter line
between Bridgwater and Taunton. This
part of the Bristol & Exeter route was
opened on 1 July 1842. The single-line
loop left the main line on the right and
connected with the Castle Cary and
Langport line at Athelney. The loop
was closed on 15 June 1964, with
Durston being closed to passengers on
5 October 1964.

Durston station is now but a
memory as Class 47 No 47840 *North
Star* speeds by with the 08.05 service
from Liverpool Lime Street to
Paignton on 1 September 2001.
GW Trust/Peter Triggs

Thornfalcon

Thornfalcon, on the Taunton to Chard branch, is seen here on 16 June 1962, as '5700' class 0-6-0PT No 3787 departs with the 8am service from Taunton to Chard Central. Thornfalcon was closed to passengers on 10 September 1962.

Improvements to the A358 road have resulted in the removal of the road bridge, and the site of the station is now covered by this industrial area; 14 April 2001. *M. J. Fox/Author*

Hatch Beauchamp

The 8am service from Taunton to Chard, hauled by '5700' class 0-6-0PT No 3736, stands at Hatch Beauchamp on 1 September 1962. The stone station was typical of those on the branch. It was closed to passengers on 10 September 1962 and to goods on 6 July 1964.

The building is now listed and is currently in use by a concrete products company, as seen here on 17 September 2001.
GW Trust/Peter Triggs

Chard (Central)

The GWR/LSWR joint station at Chard (Central) is depicted here on 22 November 1958 and on the left is 0-6-0PT No 3736 with the 1.35pm service to Taunton. On the right is 0-6-0PT No 7436 with the 1.52pm service to Chard Junction. Passenger services were withdrawn on 10 September 1962.

The station, which I understand is now listed, is in industrial use. It is not in the best of condition as can be seen on 14 April 2001. *GW Trust/Author*

Chard Junction

The short branch from Chard Central to Chard Junction was operated by BR using both former LSWR and GWR motive power. In this picture, taken at Chard Junction on 15 June 1962, the 9.34am branch service from Central is in the hands of '5700' class 0-6-0PT No 3787. This branch closed to passengers on 10 September 1962 and Chard Junction was closed on 7 March 1966. In March 2001 the line of the trackbed could still be traced and the ex-LSWR goods shed was in use for vehicle repairs, while the concrete building on the right of the first picture also still survives. *R. C. Riley/Author*

Taunton

From the footbridge west of Taunton station on 15 July 1957 '5700' class 0-6-0PT No 5721 is seen shunting empty stock for the 4.25pm service to Minehead. The station is in the background and on the right is the entrance to the steam depot which closed in October 1964.

A First Great Western HST from Plymouth to Paddington enters a vastly reduced layout at Taunton on Sunday, 15 March 2001. *R. E. Vincent/Author*

Watchet

Watchet, pictured here on 12 July 1955 with '4575' class 2-6-2T No 5522 departing with a service to Minehead. Closed to passengers on 4 January 1971, the station was reopened by the West Somerset Railway on 28 August 1986.

Crowcombe

An evening Taunton to Minehead
stopping service departs from
Crowcombe on 1 September 1951
hauled by '2251' class 0-6-0 No 2212.
The large 'M' denotes that the service
is for Minehead.

The station at Crowcombe has been
restored to its former glory by the West
Somerset Railway as seen in this view
on 20 September 2001. The signalbox,
which was officially closed on 5 March
1967, has also been restored and
reopened. *A. F. Taylor/Author*

Seen from the road bridge on 15 April
2001 '5101' class 2-6-2T No 4160
departs with an afternoon train to
Minehead. *GW Trust/Author*

Blue Anchor

Ex-GWR Mogul, '4300' class No 6398 moves slowly through Blue Anchor with an engineers train. A feature of Blue Anchor station is its close proximity to the beach.

On 20 September 2001, restored 'Manor' class 4-6-0 No 7828 *Odney Manor* enters the restored station with a Minehead to Bishops Lydeard service. The 'Manor' is just one of many ex-Barry scrapyard engines that have been restored to working order. *R. H. G. Simpson/Peter Triggs*

Minehead Shed

The loco shed and turntable at Minehead are seen here from the platform. On the turntable is a '4300' class 2-6-0. The shed was opened by the Bristol & Exeter Railway in July 1874 and was a sub-shed of Taunton. It was closed in November 1956 but the turntable continued in use long after that date.

The area around the station has altered, and today the engine sidings have been replaced by a car park. Unfortunately, the West Somerset Railway does not have the use of a turntable at present; 15 April 2001. *R. H. G. Simpson/Author*

Devon and Cornwall

The counties of Devon and Cornwall were at one time served by both the Great Western and London & South Western railways. Regional boundary changes in 1962 saw all of the former LSWR lines in Devon and Cornwall merged into the Western Region, and between 1965 and 1970 many of these were closed. Today, only the branches to Barnstaple, Exmouth and Gunnislake survive.

Of the surviving ex-GWR branches the busiest is that from St Erth to St Ives, which was opened on 1 June 1877. I took the train from Lelant Saltings to St Ives on a sunny 5 August 2001, and it would be true to say that sardines would have had more room. The Falmouth branch, which was opened on 24 August 1864, is still busy and with the construction of the new maritime museum at Falmouth Dock passenger numbers should increase. The Par to Newquay line, which was opened on 1 January 1879, is served during weekdays by Wessex Trains using Class 153 diesel units. During the summer, First Great Western operates the 'Atlantic Coast Express', a weekend HST service from Paddington to Newquay. The only other ex-Great Western branch still operating is from Liskeard to Looe, opened on 15 May 1901, and when I visited Liskeard on 11 August 2001, a rather empty Class 153 arrived from Looe.

Main line railway services in the South West are today operated by First Great Western and Virgin CrossCountry HSTs. However, in late 2001, Virgin was introducing its new 'Voyager' Class 220 trains on many routes. From 14 October 2001, intermediate services have been operated by Wessex Trains, using Class 150, 153, 156 and 158 DMUs. During 1994, a new parkway station was opened east of Plymouth, at Ivybridge. South West Trains also operates services between Penzance and Waterloo using Class 159 DMUs. Loco-hauled passenger services in the South West are now few and far between.

Freight services include oil, fertiliser, stone and china clay. The services are operated using Class 37, 60 and 66 locomotives. The through postal services are in the hands of Class 67s. Plymouth Laira is still the main servicing depot in the South West, with refuelling facilities at Penzance Long Rock, St Blazey and Exeter.

For the steam enthusiast there are now a number of preserved lines. In Cornwall the narrow gauge Launceston Steam Railway operates over a short section of the ex-LSWR Launceston to Padstow line and the Bodmin & Wenford Railway operates between Bodmin Parkway and Bodmin General and from there to Boscarne Junction. In Devon, the Paignton & Dartmouth Steam Railway runs between Paignton and Kingswear, and the South Devon Railway operates the Totnes to Buckfastleigh branch. The Plym Valley Railway has established its base at Marsh Mills on the Plymouth to Yelverton line and has recently commenced operations on a short section.

Barnstaple Victoria Road

An early Great Western view of Barnstaple Victoria Road. Standing at the single platform with a service from Taunton is what appears to be a Great Western Dean Goods 0-6-0. The station was closed to passengers on 13 June 1960, but the branch remained open for goods traffic until 5 March 1970. The second picture was taken on 5 May 1961 and shows Victoria Road in use as a goods depot.

The site of the Great Western station has now been used to widen the Victoria Road. However, the goods shed on the extreme right of both pictures still survives, and is now used for religious purposes, June 2001. *A. Goult/A. Doyle*

Cullompton

Cullompton station is seen here in 1921. The station, which was opened by the Bristol & Exeter Railway in June 1841, was rebuilt to allow for track quadrupling in December 1931. Notice the sidings on the right which use old broad gauge rails.

An obstruction narrowed the view, but the remains of the up platform can still be seen and on the right the station yard now forms part of a motorway service area; 11 August 2001. *GW Trust/Author*

Exeter St Davids

Exeter St Davids was opened by the Bristol & Exeter Railway in 1844 and was rebuilt by the Great Western circa 1910/1912. St Davids was a busy station with many inter-regional services passing through, particularly during the holiday season. Here, on 18 April 1960, '5101' class 2-6-2T No 4136 departs with the 10.50am service from Leicester London Road to Paignton and Kingswear.

Although the ornate glass façade over Platform 1 has now been removed, as has the through centre line, otherwise the station has changed little. On 11 August 2001 Class 150 No 150239 arrives with the 11.07 Wales & West service from Barnstaple to Exmouth. *GW Trust/Author*

Exeter St Thomas

The other former Great Western station in Exeter is St Thomas, depicted here in 1921. The station is constructed on a viaduct and was opened by the South Devon Railway in May 1846. The old SDR entrance building was let as shops in 1959, and around this time the up platform was lengthened.

The overall roof was removed during the 1970s, but the downside station entrance building survives and is seen here on 4 August 2001 as a First Great Western Class 47 speeds through with a Paddington to Penzance Motorail service. *GW Trust/Author*

Christow

'5700' class 0-6-0PT No 7716 arrives at Christow on 7 December 1957 with the 12.45pm service from Exeter to Newton Abbot. The station stood on the Heathfield to Exeter branch and was closed to passengers on 9 June 1958. The branch was closed completely when the line was cut due to flooding on 30 September 1960.

The present view is best seen from the road overbridge as photographed on 11 August 2001. The station building and platforms still remain as part of a private house and the trackbed is now a lawn. *GW Trust/Author*

Bovey

'5101' class 2-6-2T No 4176 stands at Bovey on 7 December 1957 with the 2.15pm service to Newton Abbot comprising one coach. The local pick-up goods is just departing behind the Prairie tank. The Moretonhampstead branch was opened by the South Devon Railway on 4 July 1866 and passenger services were withdrawn on 2 March 1959.

Trusham

'517' class 0-4-2T enters Trusham with a Newton Abbot to Exeter via Heathfield service. The Teign Valley branch was closed to passengers on 9 June 1958, but remained open as far as Trusham for goods traffic until 5 April 1965.

The road overbridge is still in situ, but the trackbed is now too overgrown for a picture, hence the slightly different angle. On 11 August 2001 the station building has been renovated and is in use as a holiday home. The caravan probably provides extra accommodation. *GW Trust/Author*

On 4 August 2001, the trackbed forms part of the main road to Moretonhampstead but the goods shed and station buildings survive. The area behind the station buildings is now covered by retirement flats. *GW Trust/Author*

Lustleigh

Lustleigh was also situated on the Moretonhampstead branch and is pictured here in the early 1920s as a '517' class 0-4-2T arrives with a branch service from Newton Abbot. Lustleigh was closed to passengers on 2 March 1959.

Since closure, the station has been converted to a private residence and is seen here on 4 August 2001. *GW Trust/Author*

Dawlish

Dawlish was opened by the South Devon Railway in 1846 and a 'Star' class 4-6-0 is seen pulling into the station circa 1908. This view shows the interesting roof canopy which was installed on both up and down platforms. Because of its close proximity to the sea the station and track regularly suffer storm damage during the winter months.

The station was rebuilt by the Great Western during the 1930s, and is seen here in June 2001 as Class 150 No 150243 arrives with a Plymouth to Bristol service. *GW Trust/A. E. Doyle*

Brixham

The terminus station at Brixham, Devon, is pictured here on 9 July 1953. I have chosen this photograph without a train to show as much of the station detail as possible. The two-mile broad gauge branch from Churston to Brixham was opened on 28 February 1868.

Converted to standard gauge in May 1892, it was closed to all traffic on 13 May 1963. The site is now covered by a housing development.
GW Trust/A. E. Doyle

Ashburton shed

The steam locomotive depot at Ashburton in June 1954. Opened by the South Devon Railway in 1872, this former broad gauge shed was for many years a sub-shed of Newton Abbot. It was closed in November 1958.

Totnes

Totnes is shown here in the 1920s, with '2721' class 0-6-0PT No 2783 on shunting duty, and marshalling a short goods service on the up main line. The station was opened by the South Devon Railway on 20 July 1847. The overall roof sections on the up and down platforms date from broad gauge days and were removed during station rebuilding in 1923. No 2783 was built at Swindon as a saddle tank in January 1901, converted to a pannier tank in October 1913 and withdrawn from service in November 1947. The station underwent further change in 1954 when the entrance building on the down platform was burned down.

In recent years, the station has been refurbished and on 11 August 2001 an HST on the 11.33 First Great Western service from Paddington to Penzance rushes through. *GW Trust/Author*

Luckily, the shed survived and is seen here on 4 August 2001 in industrial use, the shed itself is used by a joinery firm, and the visually appalling extension houses an engineering company. *GW Trust/Author*

123

Kingsbridge

An early postcard view of the station at Kingsbridge depicting the scene shortly after the arrival of the branch service from Brent, hauled by '517' class 0-4-2T. The Kingsbridge branch was opened by the Great Western on 19 December 1893 and closed on 16 September 1963.

The station building still survives amidst a rather untidy industrial estate. The station approach road has been swallowed up under the widened A379; 11 August 2001. *GW Trust/Author*

Ivybridge

Ivybridge, looking east; the station stood just to the west of Ivybridge Viaduct. The picture is undated, but judging by the condition of the station was probably taken around its closure date of 2 March 1959.

In July 1994 a new parkway station was opened, but unfortunately, not on the site of the old station, as locals will tell you that the new station is in the wrong place and sees little use. Running through a heavy shower at Ivybridge Parkway on 4 August 2001 is an HST on a First Great Western service from Paddington to Plymouth. The platforms here are staggered with the up platform west of the down platform and a large steel footbridge links both with the car park. *GW Trust/Author*

Yelverton

'1400' class 0-4-2T No 1408 stands at Yelverton with the 10.44am service from Plymouth and forming the 11.16am from Yelverton to Tavistock, on a wet 20 December 1955. Yelverton was opened on 1 May 1885. Curving away to the left is the Princetown branch and standing in the platform is the 11.20am to Princetown, hauled by '4500' class 2-6-2T No 4568 (not in view). The Princetown branch was closed on 5 March 1956 but Yelverton remained open until 31 December 1962, on which date the former GWR Plym Valley line from Plymouth to Tavistock South was closed.

Since that date the whole station area has been swallowed up by undergrowth. The station site is privately owned and has been designated a nature reserve. With the owner's permission, I climbed the barbed wire fence on to what was the down platform. Literally fighting my way through the wild rose bushes, shrubs and trees along a very damp trackbed, I found the end of the up platform and took this picture. You can just make it out on the left. My wife and the landowner, who were both watching, were highly amused at my safari; 11 August 2001.
Hugh Ballantyne/Author

Plymouth North Road

The end of the main up platform at Plymouth North Road on 5 May 1959. From left to right are 'County' class 4-6-0 No 1009 *County of Carmarthen* on an up parcels, '1400' class 0-4-2T No 1471, and 'Castle' class 4-6-0 No 5069 *Isambard Kingdom Brunel* on the 'Brunel Centenarian' special. The station at Plymouth North Road was partially reconstructed by the Great Western during 1939, but World War 2 curtailed further work and the rebuilding was not finally completed until 26 March 1962.

Yealmpton

A view of Yealmpton station taken on 9 July 1953. The branch from Plymstock Junction to Yealmpton was opened for passenger traffic on 17 January 1898. The station closed on 7 July 1930, but was reopened for passengers on 3 November 1941. Passenger traffic was withdrawn for good on 6 October 1947, and replaced by a bus service. However, the branch remained open for goods traffic until 29 February 1960 and was lifted during 1962.

The site of the station, as depicted on 11 August 2001, is now covered by a housing estate entered via Riverside Walk. A small notice on the wall on the right explains to the passer-by that this was once the site of Yealmpton station.

The station entrance is dominated by the 1962 tower block that also forms part of the station building. Class 67 No 67026 heads a Royal Mail service while, right, an HST arrives with an up First Great Western service from Penzance to London on 11 August 2001.
GW Trust/Author

Saltash

Saltash is the first station on the main line west of the Royal Albert Bridge and was opened on 4 May 1859. On 7 August 1958, the 1.20pm service from Penzance to Paddington passes through the station hauled by 'Modified Hall' 4-6-0 No 7916 *Mobberley Hall*. The station, which prior to the opening of the adjacent roadbridge, had 30 services a day to Plymouth, is now unstaffed and served by Wessex Trains services. The up entrance building, which was constructed when the station was rebuilt in 1880, survives but is boarded up.

A First Great Western HST passes through Saltash on 4 August 2001 with the 13.28 service from Penzance to Paddington. The footbridge has now gone and passengers must cross the line by the road bridge. *GW Trust/Author*

Liskeard

Liskeard is seen here in the early part of the last century as an up semi-fast service arrives from Penzance hauled by a 'Bulldog' class 4-4-0. Notice the porters carrying passengers' luggage, a service that has all but disappeared on today's railway.

The down platform building has been removed and replaced with a concrete shelter, and a new extension has been built on to the high level entrance, but many other areas are unchanged; 11 August 2001. *GW Trust/Author*

Bodmin Road

A view from the east end of Bodmin Road in 1922. On the right are the sidings and platform for the branch to Bodmin General. Bodmin Road became Bodmin Parkway on 1 November 1983.

Looking from the same spot on 4 August 2001, an HST arrives at Bodmin Parkway with the 15.05 First Great Western service from Penzance to Paddington. Both water towers have long gone, but the branch is still open and operated by the Bodmin & Wenford Railway. *GW Trust/Author*

Bodmin General

This view of Bodmin General on 4 August 1958 shows '4575' class 2-6-2T No 5557 running round the 10.10am arrival from Bodmin Road; the 2-6-2T will take the train on to Wadebridge. The signalbox was closed on 17 December 1967 and was demolished.

Bodmin General

The attractive stone station at Bodmin General is seen here in June 1925. The 3½- mile branch from Bodmin General to Bodmin Road (now Bodmin Parkway) was opened by the Great Western on 27 May 1887. A second branch from Bodmin General, which connected with the LSWR's Bodmin & Wadebridge line at Boscarne Junction, was opened on 3 September 1888. Passenger services between Bodmin General and Bodmin Road were withdrawn on 30 January 1966, but the branch remained open for goods traffic until September 1983.

Bodmin General is now the headquarters of the Bodmin & Wenford Railway which has restored passenger services from there to both Bodmin Parkway and Boscarne Junction. Seen from the platform, not the track, on 4 August 2001, the sidings and platform are full of preserved stock. On the right are ex-BR Class 08 No D3559 and Class 33 No 33110. *GW Trust/Author*

In the same spot on 4 August 2001, a new locomotive shed stands on the site of the old goods shed. The signalbox has been rebuilt to the original specification using 'spare parts' from other closed boxes and is now back in full operating order. *GW Trust/Author*

Lostwithiel

The up 'Cornishman', the 10.30am
service from Penzance to
Wolverhampton, speeds through
Lostwithiel on 4 August 1958, hauled
by 'Hall' class 4-6-0 No 6940
Didlington Hall. Lostwithiel was the
junction for Fowey branch services
which departed from the bay on the left.
   On 8 August 2001, Class 158
No 158827 arrives at Lostwithiel with
the 11.40 Alphaline service from
Penzance to Cardiff Central.
GW Trust/Author

Lostwithiel

Looking east, on 4 August 1958, 'Modified Hall' class 4-6-0 No 7925 *Westol Hall* arrives at Lostwithiel with the 11.5am service from Plymouth to Penzance, while standing in the bay is '1400' class 0-4-2T No 1419 with the 12.27pm service to Fowey.

The view in the down direction on 8 August 2001 sees Class 158 No 158864 arriving with the 08.00 Alphaline service from Cardiff Central to Penzance. The old station buildings and the footbridge have long gone. The Fowey bay is now used as a siding for china clay traffic. In the centre distance is the ex-GWR signalbox, which is still in operation and also controls the adjacent crossing.
GW Trust/Author

Fowey

The branch from Lostwithiel to Fowey was opened as a mineral railway on 1 June 1869. It closed on 1 January 1880 but was reopened for passenger traffic by the Great Western on 16 September 1895. The branch was important for china clay traffic as Fowey was the principal china clay port in Cornwall. The small terminus station is seen here on 4 August 1958 with 0-4-2T No 1419 waiting to depart with the 1.45pm service to Lostwithiel. The branch was closed to passenger traffic on 4 January 1965.

The Fowey branch, which today is still used by china clay trains, terminates at Carne Point. The site of the station at Fowey is now covered by a road into the port and the local library on the right. The slight change of angle avoids the vegetation and shows the remains of the station building on the left; 8 August 2001. *GW Trust/Author*

Par

A view of Par station taken from the adjacent road overbridge in 1922. The main line to the west is on the left and on the right is the platform for services to Newquay.

St Blazey Shed

A view of St Blazey shed in 1936 with a pair of Great Western 0-6-0PTs. The shed was opened by the GWR in around 1872 and comprised a brick-built semi-roundhouse with nine roads. It was closed to steam in April 1962 but continued in use as a diesel depot until 25 April 1987.

The building, which is Grade 2 listed, is seen here on 8 August 2001 and is currently being used for the manufacture of furniture. I have widened the view to show the small refuelling depot at St Blazey that replaced the old shed during 1987. Engines at the refuelling depot on the date visited were Nos 08950, 08953, 60073, 66144 and 67025.
GW Trust/Author

On 8 August 2001, a First Great Western HST service to Penzance runs through the station. The building on the up platform has been removed and replaced by a shelter and part of the goods yard is in industrial use, but otherwise there are few obvious changes. *GW Trust/Author*

Perranporth

Perranporth stood on the branch from Chacewater to Newquay. The first section, from Chacewater to Perranporth, was opened on 6 July 1903 and then to Newquay, on 2 January 1905. The station is seen here on 3 August 1959 with '4575' class 2-6-2T No 5539 on the 4pm service from Newquay. The station comprised an island platform with access via a subway. Passenger services were withdrawn on 4 February 1963.

Nothing now remains of the station and as can be seen on 8 August 2001, the station site and yard are now covered by a number of small industrial units. *GW Trust/Author*

St Austell

A view from the road bridge at St Austell: on the right, shunting in the yard is '5700' class 0-6-0PT and standing in the up platform is what appears to be a 'City' class 4-4-0 with an up semi-fast service.

Newquay

'4575' class 2-6-2T No 5539 stands at Platform 2 at Newquay on 3 August 1958 after arriving with the 4.35pm service from Perranporth. The stock can be seen beyond the locomotive. The station at this time had two main platforms and a bay.

Currently, services use the old Newquay Railway, which opened for passengers from the junction at Par on 20 June 1876. The one platform now in use at Newquay has been shortened to provide a larger waiting area, and is visible in this picture on 8 August 2001. Just arrived with the 08.19 service from Par is Wales & West Class 153 No 153362. On summer Saturdays Newquay is also served by the First Great Western 11.06 HST service from Paddington, the 'Atlantic Coast Express'. *GW Trust/Author*

On a sunny 8 August 2001, Class 158 No 158868 arrives as the 11.00 Wales & West service from Cardiff to Penzance. The sidings on the right were once used by Motorail trains from Kensington Olympia. The service started on 24 May 1966 and was withdrawn in September 1982. Today, the two remaining sidings have been shortened and appear to be unused. *GW Trust/Author*

Burngullow

The scene from the road overbridge at Burngullow in 1922. This is the second station here and was opened on 1 August 1901. The ex-Cornwall Railway station which was situated approximately quarter of a mile further east was closed on the same date. The branch on the right was opened as far as Drinnick Mill by the Newquay & West Cornwall Railway on 1 July 1869 and was extended to St Dennis on 1 June 1874. The branch was taken over by the GWR on 1 October 1877. The small engine shed on the right was opened on 1 July 1869. It was officially closed in March 1906, but was not demolished until 1929. The station at Burngullow was closed to passengers on 14 September 1931.

Looking down from the same spot nothing now remains of the Great Western station. However, the old Cornwall Railway stationmaster's house is still in use as a private residence. On 8 August 2001, Class 150 No 150234 runs past with the 10.12 Wales & West service from Penzance to Cardiff Central. The main line was singled between Burngullow and Probus on 4 October 1986 and the branch is still in use as far as Kernick, serving a number of china clay workings en route. *GW Trust/Author*

Truro

The 7.30am service from Penzance to Manchester, hauled by 'Castle' class 4-6-0 No 4095 *Harlech Castle* stands in the up relief platform at Truro on 6 August 1958. Truro is the junction station for the branch to Falmouth.

To re-create the shot on the same date 43 years later, I stood on the same spot on 6 August 2001 but unfortunately it was a foul day and raining heavily. The up relief platform is devoid of track as is the adjacent yard, which is now a car park, and also houses some commercial units. The Class 158 DMU has arrived with the 11.40 Alphaline service from Penzance to Cardiff. *GW Trust/Author*

Falmouth

Falmouth is seen here on 3 August 1958 with the 9.51am service just arrived from Truro behind '4575' class 2-6-2T No 5515. The station, which was opened by the Cornwall Railway on 24 August 1863, once boasted an overall roof. This was removed in 1956 and replaced by the canopy seen here. On 7 December 1970, a new station was opened nearer the town using concrete parts from the closed Perranporth Beach Halt, and the old station was closed. However, on 5 May 1975 the down platform was reopened as Falmouth, with the replacement town station renamed The Dell.

Falmouth has been converted into a parkway station and the new car park can be seen on the left. On 9 August 2001, Wales & West Class 150 No 150247 arrives with the branch service from Truro. Passenger traffic over the line should increase with the opening of the new National Maritime Museum, which was under construction at the time of writing. *GW Trust/Author*

Redruth

A view from above the short tunnel at Redruth in 1906. Entering the station with an up stopping service is what appears to be a Great Western '4400' class 2-6-2 with its numberplate on the side tank. Beyond the station is Redruth Viaduct.

Redruth Drump Lane Goods

This excellent view shows the Great Western goods yard at Drump Lane, Redruth. Standing on the yard siding is 'Duke' class 4-4-0 No 3291 *Tregenna*. Drump Lane was opened on 17 June 1912 and closed during the 1970s. The sidings were lifted in June 1986. Drump Lane signalbox, seen here on the right, was closed on 12 June 1986.

Looking down from the footbridge on 5 August 2001, only the goods shed remains from the yard. *GW Trust/Author*

It is difficult to get exactly the same position today; the small yard on the left is now in industrial use. The west yard goods shed has gone and is now the station car park. The station is served by Wessex Trains services from Plymouth to Penzance; 5 August 2001. *GW Trust/Author*

Gwinear Road

Gwinear Road was the junction station for the Helston branch, and the branch platform is on the right. The station is seen here on 7 August 1958 as '4500' class 2-6-2T No 4563 runs through the station in preparation for working the branch service. Gwinear Road was closed on 5 October 1964.

Only the down platform survives in this picture taken on 5 August 2001.The crossing is now the automatic gate type, and the Helston branch trackbed is overgrown. Two trains passed through in the short time I was there, but I did not include them as each would have obscured the view of the down platform and crossing.
GW Trust/Author

Helston

The terminus at Helston is seen here on 7 August 1958. Standing in the platform is 2-6-2T No 4563 with the 7pm service to Gwinear Road. The branch was opened by the Helston Railway Company on 9 May 1887. The intention was to continue the branch through to The Lizard, but because of cost this was soon abandoned. Helston was closed to passengers on 3 November 1962, and to goods traffic two years later. It was the first Cornish branch to be closed to passengers.

The road to the station now leads into a housing estate and the only surviving evidence of a railway is the goods shed, which is in private use, seen on the left in both pictures, the latter taken on 5 August 2001. *GW Trust/Author*

The Lizard

Motorised transport at The Lizard. The Great Western introduced a motor bus service between Helston and The Lizard on Monday, 17 August 1903. In this view, taken on that day outside Hill's Hotel, the GWR motor bus, registration AF 66, is on the right.

On 5 August 2001, Hill's Hotel is now The Top House and cars occupy the old bus terminus. The stable building on the right is now a gift shop and run by a descendant of the Hill family. *GW Trust/Author*

St Erth

'Grange' class 4-6-0 No 6845 *Paviland Grange* departs from St Erth on 6 April 1960 with the 1.35pm broccoli train from Ponsandane. St Erth is the junction for the St Ives branch.

On a very sunny 5 August 2001, Class 159 No 159001 arrives with the 14.14 South West Trains service from Penzance to London Waterloo. Standing in the bay on the right is the shuttle service to St Ives.
P. Treloar/Author

Penzance

Journey's end. The 12 noon express from Paddington hauled by 'Bulldog' class 4-4-0 No 3348 stands at Penzance on 11 March 1919. The station was opened by the West Cornwall Railway on 11 March 1852. It was rebuilt by the Great Western in November 1880 and enlarged again in 1939 to provide four platforms.

St Ives

The 11.15am service from St Erth stands at St Ives on a wet 2 August 1958. '4500' class 2-6-2T No 4547 seems to have a variety of lamps and oil cans on its front running plate. The stock will form the 11.50am service back to St Erth; one hopes the departing passengers had had some sunny days. The St Ives branch was opened by the West Cornwall Railway on 1 June 1877 and was the last broad gauge line to be built. If you listen to Flanders & Swann's 'Slow Train' you might believe that trains are no more from St Erth to St Ives, but that is not the case.

Although the old station has now gone, a new single platform was opened on 21 May 1971 to serve the town. Because of traffic congestion in St Ives many visitors now travel in by train, using the parkway station at Lelant Saltings. That is what I did on 5 August 2001, arriving on Class 153 No 153308. *GW Trust/Author*

Seen from the same spot on 5 August 2001, South West Trains Class 159 No 159001 is stabled at Platform 3 after working in on the previous day with a service from Waterloo. Today, Virgin CrossCountry and First Great Western HST services generally arrive and depart from Platforms 1 and 2.
LCGB Ken Nunn Collection/Author

Section 4 - The Midlands, Cotswolds and Border Counties

Gloucestershire, Shropshire, Warwickshire, the West Midlands, Oxfordshire and Wiltshire, Herefordshire and Worcestershire

One of the bright features of the ex-Great Western lines in the Midlands is the resurgence of the main line from London to Birmingham. Considerable investment by Chiltern Railways has seen refurbishment work undertaken at Banbury, Solihull, Dorridge and Birmingham Snow Hill, and the opening of a new £4.2 million station at Warwick Parkway in February 2000. The introduction of the new 'Clubman' trains has resulted in an increase in passenger services from a September 1994 weekly total of 1,305 to 1,719 in May 2001.

Trains to Worcester and Hereford now depart from Birmingham Snow Hill with the reinstatement of the link to Smethick West. The old Great Western route from Birmingham to Wolverhampton is now used by the new Midland Metro tram system which was opened on 31 May 1999.

Services over the ex-GWR main line from Snow Hill to London are operated by Chiltern Railways using Class 165 and 168 DMUs. First Great Western operates HSTs on its service from Paddington to Cheltenham, and Paddington to Worcester and Hereford. The Cotswold line from Oxford to Worcester has seen some growth in traffic in recent years, but is still the Cinderella when it comes to meaningful investment.

Local services in the Midlands and Borders are operated by Central Trains and Wales & Borders using mainly Class 150, 156, 158 and now 170 units. The same companies also operate services to Shrewsbury and Chester. Between Hooton and Birkenhead Central (the Great Western & Birkenhead joint station at Birkenhead Woodside was closed in 1967) the line is electrified and operated by Arriva Merseyside.

The whole of the West Midlands and Border areas still sees a considerable amount of freight traffic, and once again, we have mixed freight trains. Many of these services now use the new Class 66 locomotives, but Classes 37, 47, 56 and 60 can still be seen on a regular basis.

The Midlands steam enthusiast is well catered for with three former Great Western lines being operated by railway preservation societies. Possibly the country's premier preserved line, the Severn Valley, operates a regular passenger service between Kidderminster and Bridgnorth. The Gloucestershire Warwickshire Railway goes from strength to strength and has extended its route from Toddington to Gotherington, and in 2003 will open through to Cheltenham Racecourse station. The Dean Forest Railway currently operates services from Lydney Junction to Norchard, with plans to extend to Park End. The City of Birmingham has its own railway centre at Tyseley where a number of ex-Great Western locomotives are kept and maintained on the site of the old steam depot. The adjacent diesel depot is the main servicing and repair shop for Central Trains DMUs.

For continuity, some Oxfordshire and Wiltshire locations have been included in this section.

South Cerney

The ex-M&SWJR station at South Cerney is depicted in October 1961, shortly after closure. The station opened as Cerney & Ashton Keynes but was renamed South Cerney on 1 July 1924. Although it was closed to passengers on 11 September 1961, it remained open for goods traffic until 1 July 1963.

I visited South Cerney on 11 March 2001 and found a housing estate now stands on the site of the station. The road overbridge, shown in the first picture, can just be seen in the distance. *GW Trust/Author*

Cricklade

Cricklade station, seen here in July 1958, was on the Midland & South Western Junction route from Cheltenham to Andover. The line was closed to passengers on 11 September 1961, but remained open for some goods traffic until 1 July 1963. This station stood derelict for a number of years after closure until the whole lot was swept away to allow for new road and housing developments.

Photographed from the top of the old railway embankment on 11 March 2001, this view shows the scene as it has been in recent times. *GW Trust/Author*

Hanborough

'Castle' class 4-6-0 No 7027 *Thornbury Castle* passes Handborough on 14 May 1962 with an up Worcester service. This was originally known as Handborough Junction when the Oxford, Worcester & Wolverhampton Railway operated its through service from Worcester to Euston in 1854, and for a time the station even had its own refreshment room.

The remains of the down platform can be seen here on 10 April 2001. The line is single at this point and all services use the up platform. The Oxford Bus Museum now occupies the old goods yard. Hanborough, the 'D' of which was dropped from the name by British Rail in 1993, is in close proximity to Witney, and with improved parking facilities, would make a good park-and-ride station for commuters to Oxford.

Chipping Norton

Watched by the driver, the fireman climbs down from the front of '4575' class 2-6-2T No 5530 as it waits to depart from Chipping Norton with a service to Kingham on 3 July 1954. Through passenger services were withdrawn between Banbury and Kingham on 4 June 1951, after which date Chipping Norton became the terminus of the branch. Passenger services between Kingham and Chipping Norton were withdrawn on 3 December 1962.

Charlbury

A down Worcester and Hereford service hauled by 'Castle' class 4-6-0 No 7007 *Great Western* pulls in to Charlbury during the 1950s. The station building is a standard Brunel design, but probably due to cost was built of wood rather than stone.

The down platform was taken out of use during February 1971 when the down track was removed. The signalbox was closed on 24 February 1971. Much rationalisation has taken place, but the station building shows little change in this 10 April 2001 view, while the up platform was extended during 1968. Notice how well kept the station is in both pictures. *GW Trust/Author*

A builders' supply merchant now occupies the site of Chipping Norton station and the station goods yard is now the Station Industrial Site as depicted on 14 April 2001. The road overbridge is still in situ and the entrance to Chipping Norton Tunnel beyond the bridge, can still be seen. *GW Trust/Author*

Bloxham

The Railway Enthusiast Club 'South Midlander' special stops at Bloxham on the line from Kingham to King's Sutton on 24 April 1955. Bloxham was opened by the Banbury & Cheltenham Direct Railway on 6 April 1887. Passenger services were withdrawn between Banbury and Chipping Norton on 4 June 1951, but the line from Bloxham to Adderbury remained open for goods traffic until 4 November 1963.

The remains of the road overbridge are still in situ, and seen from the same spot on 10 April 2001 new houses now occupy the site of the station. *GW Trust/Author*

Moreton-in-Marsh

The 3.33pm (SO) stopping train from Oxford to Worcester, hauled by 'Hall' class 4-6-0 No 6910 *Gossington Hall*, stands at Moreton-in-Marsh on 16 May 1964. This was the junction for the branch to Shipston-on-Stour which was closed to passengers on 8 July 1929 and to goods on 2 May 1960.

Seen from the footbridge on a sunny 23 October 2001, Class 166 No 166204 arrives with the 11.17 service to Hereford. The signalbox here is still in operation for token exchange. The old Shipston branch platform is on the left. *M. C. Burdge/Author*

Aston Magna

Just north of Moreton-in-Marsh was the siding at Aston Magna. In this undated but *c*1920s picture, a Dean Goods 0-6-0 passes Aston Magna signalbox with a down goods service. The siding on the left served Gloucestershire Brick & Tile Co, which was removed in 1957. The signalbox, which was opened on 15 September 1902, closed on 15 December 1946.

The view from the road bridge on 23 October 2001 sees Class 165 No 165110 passing with the 12.37 service from Moreton-in-Marsh to Hereford. *GW Trust/Author*

Honeybourne Junction

The down 'Cathedrals Express', hauled by 'Castle' class 4-6-0 No 5001 *Llandovery Castle*, passes through Honeybourne Junction in August 1961. Honeybourne Junction once boasted four platforms and two bays, with trains to Worcester, Oxford and London, and to Stratford-on-Avon, Warwick and Cheltenham. Passenger services to Cheltenham were withdrawn on 7 March 1960 and to Stratford-on-Avon on 3 January 1966, with Honeybourne Junction station closing to passengers on 5 May 1969. The main line through Honeybourne was singled, and the area rationalised on 20 September 1971.

Evesham

An up goods service from the Ashchurch line, hauled by 'Hall' class 4-6-0 No 4971 *Stanway Hall*, arrives to take water at Evesham on 14 April 1962. The ex-Midland Railway station, out of view on the left, was closed to passengers on 17 June 1963. Goods services between Evesham and the Ministry of Defence siding at Ashchurch were withdrawn on 9 September 1963.

Evesham is today one of the passing points on the Cotswold line between Oxford and Worcester. The south signalbox, seen in the first picture, closed on 15 March 1957 and was replaced by a new north box which is still open. Seen from the road bridge on 18 July 2001, Class 166 No 166201 departs with a Thames Trains service from Worcester Shrub Hill to Oxford.
M. Mensing/Author

Honeybourne is now a pale shadow of what was once quite a busy railway junction with goods yards and sidings, and at one time, an engine shed. The platform on the right was opened on 25 May 1981 and is served by Thames Trains stopping services. As can be seen, part of the island platform remains, but all of the sidings and yards have now been removed; 18 July 2001.
GW Trust/Author

Worcester Shrub Hill

The 5.35pm service from Hereford to Paddington arrives at Worcester Shrub Hill on 20 April 1961 behind 'Hall' class 4-6-0 No 4913 *Baglan Hall*.

On 26 July 2001, Class 156 No 156417 waits to leave with the 12.26 Central Trains service from Cardiff to Nottingham. The through centre line is now a siding and the large upside building has been removed. *M. Mensing/Author*

Malvern Link

The 3.50pm service from Malvern Wells to Worcester comprises '4800' class 0-4-2T No 4818 and auto-coach No 43 which stands in the up platform at Malvern Link on 4 June 1937.

The station has been reduced to the minimum, the only building to survive being the old stationmaster's house on the right, which is now a private residence. Two-car Class 150 No 150125 arrives forming the 09.04 service from Stourbridge Junction to Hereford on 18 July 2001. *GW Trust/Author*

Worcester Foregate Street

'7200' class 2-8-2T No 7220 passes through Worcester Foregate Street with an up goods train on 6 September 1958. This station is built on a viaduct, and with so little room the signalbox was constructed above the station footbridge. The box, which was installed in 1884, was closed on 16 August 1959, and both it and the footbridge have now been removed. The down platform awning has also been shortened.

Class 150 No 150105 arrives with a service from Malvern to Birmingham Snow Hill on 26 July 2001.
GW Trust/Author

Bromyard

The 10.50am service to Worcester, hauled by '5700' class 0-6-0PT No 7707, waits at Bromyard on 6 September 1958. The first section of the Worcester, Bromyard & Leominster Railway, between Bransford Road Junction and Bromyard, was opened on 22 October 1877. The section from Bromyard through to Leominster was not completed until 1 September 1897. Bromyard became the terminus of the branch from Worcester with the closure of the Bromyard to Leominster section in 1952.

Passenger services were withdrawn on 7 September 1964 and the line closed. The site of the station is now covered by the Hydro Automotive Structures factory and a road has been built on the trackbed, but the road overbridge remains; photographed on 18 July 2001. *GW Trust/Author*

Leominster

Leominster stands on the ex-GW & LNWR joint line from Hereford to Craven Arms and is pictured here on 5 September 1958. In the background, a goods service hauled by '7400' class 0-6-0PT No 7437 takes the station avoiding line. The platform for Bromyard branch services was behind the main line platform on the right. The large signalbox was opened in 1881 and closed on 18 October 1964. Passenger and goods services between Leominster and Bromyard were withdrawn on 15 September 1952.

On 5 June 2001, a Class 158 DMU speeds through Leominster with a Cardiff to Manchester service. The main entrance building is pretty much intact, but the buildings on Platform 2 have been replaced with a shelter. *GW Trust/Author*

Newent

The 1.30pm Ledbury to Gloucester Central service, worked by '4500' class 2-6-2T No 4573, arrives at Newent on 6 September 1958. The Ledbury to Gloucester branch was opened on 27 July 1885. Newent was closed to passengers on 13 July 1959 and to goods on 1 June 1964.

It is difficult to take a picture from the same spot due to the number of trees that have grown on the site. In this picture taken on 5 June 2001, the entrance road to the station can be seen on the right. The two platforms are still in situ beyond the dumped car and in the small wood that has now taken over the station area. *GW Trust/Author*

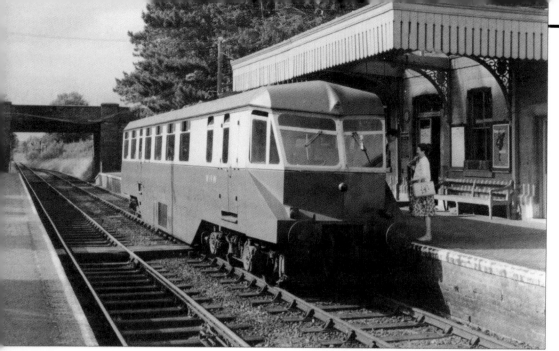

Dymock

Diesel railcar No W19W stands at Dymock with 5.25pm service to Ledbury on 11 July 1959, the last day of passenger services over the branch. The line remained open for goods traffic until 1 June 1964.

The site of Dymock station is now covered by retirement flats. The road bridge provides the reference point in this picture taken on 18 July 2001, and the edge of the platform can just be seen in the centre foreground. *Hugh Ballantyne/ Author*

Ross-on-Wye

'4300' class 2-6-0 No 5355 arrives at Ross-on-Wye on 10 June 1957 with the 4.25pm service from Hereford to Gloucester. Opened by the Hereford, Ross & Gloucester Railway on 1 June 1855, passenger services between Hereford and Gloucester were withdrawn on 2 November 1964 and on the same date Ross-on-Wye station was closed. Goods services survived until 1 November 1965.

Today, the site forms part of the Station Industrial Estate and the goods shed has been restored. It is pictured here on 5 June 2001 and shows the large coloured mural depicting 2-6-2T No 5541. *GW Trust/Author*

Ross-on-Wye Shed

Another former railway building that is still in use at Ross-on-Wye is the single-road engine shed. It is seen here on 3 June 1959, with the sole occupant, 0-6-0PT No 7437. The shed, which dates from around 1871, was for many years a sub-shed to Hereford. It closed in October 1963.

The building is now listed and has been restored. On 5 June 2001 it was in use as a home and garden centre. The road in the foreground serves the Station Industrial Estate, and behind the shed is the Ross-on-Wye bypass. *GW Trust/Author*

Upper Lydbrook

Upper Lydbrook, in the Forest of Dean, is pictured here on 21 November 1959. The Severn & Wye Joint line, which ran from Lydbrook Junction to Serridge Junction, was closed to passengers on 8 July 1929, but remained open for goods traffic until 30 January 1956. Part of the station can be seen on the right.

Today, the trackbed can be traced and part of the platform still remains amid the trees. The tower of Upper Lydbrook parish church (built 1851), although partially obscured by trees in this photograph, also gives a good reference point; 5 June 2001. *GW Trust/Author*

Monmouth Troy

The two-coach 12.45pm service to Ross-on-Wye, hauled by '1400' class 0-4-2T No 1455 stands at Monmouth Troy on 10 June 1957. This was once a busy station with services to Ross-on-Wye, Chepstow and Pontypool Road but was closed to passengers on 2 November 1964.

Standing on about the same spot on 5 June 2001, nothing recognisable remains of Monmouth Troy. New housing has been built over what was the station entrance and yard. The tunnel is still in situ, but is now hidden by the trees. However, the station building survives, having been rebuilt at Winchcombe on the Gloucestershire Warwickshire Railway.
GW Trust/Author

Tintern

The 11.50am service from Monmouth Troy to Newport, headed by '5700' class 0-6-0PT No 7714, calls at Tintern on 3 January 1959. Tintern was the main passing point on the Wye Valley branch from Chepstow to Ross. The Wye Valley Railway was opened on 1 November 1876. A particularly scenic route, it was unfortunately closed to passengers on 5 January 1959.

The station and signalbox survive and today form part of a visitor centre. A couple of railway coaches are used for refreshments and a small museum; 5 June 2001. *GW Trust/Author*

Lydney Town

Lydney Town was served by auto-train
services from Lydney Junction and
Berkeley Road. Passenger services
were withdrawn on 26 October 1960.
The line remained open for goods
traffic until 1 August 1967. The station
is pictured here on 6 September 1958
as '1400' class 0-4-2T No 1428
prepares to depart with the 5.44pm
service to Berkeley Road.

The line has been taken over by the
Dean Forest Railway which operates
passenger services between Lydney
Junction and Norchard. A new station
at Lydney Town, seen here in the centre
distance on 5 June 2001, was opened
on 22 April the same year by the town
mayor, David Clarke. *GW Trust/Author*

Coleford

The ex-Severn & Wye station at
Coleford is pictured here in 1948.
Opened on 1 September 1883, this
was the terminus of the branch from
Parkend. Passenger traffic was
withdrawn on 8 June 1929, but the
branch remained open for goods traffic
until 1 August 1967.

A road now crosses the site of the
station, but the goods shed has survived
and is now used as a railway museum,
which is situated behind the trees on the
left. The church tower in the first picture
provides a reference point, but is now
partially obscured by the trees; 5 June
2001. *GW Trust/Author*

Cinderford

The 2.35pm service from Gloucester Central hauled by BR-built '1600' class 0-6-0PT No 1639 stands at Cinderford on 6 September 1958. Passenger services were withdrawn on 3 November 1958, but the branch remained open for goods until 1 August 1967.

The site of the station is now covered by a housing estate called the Keelings and a plaque on one of the houses explains why; 5 June 2001.
GW Trust/Author

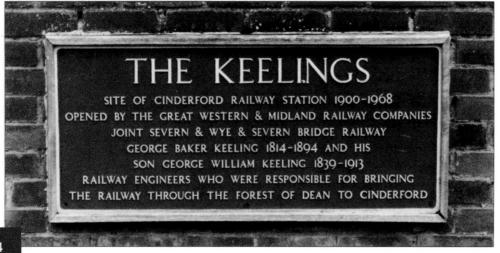

THE KEELINGS
SITE OF CINDERFORD RAILWAY STATION 1900-1968
OPENED BY THE GREAT WESTERN & MIDLAND RAILWAY COMPANIES
JOINT SEVERN & WYE & SEVERN BRIDGE RAILWAY
GEORGE BAKER KEELING 1814-1894 AND HIS
SON GEORGE WILLIAM KEELING 1839-1913
RAILWAY ENGINEERS WHO WERE RESPONSIBLE FOR BRINGING
THE RAILWAY THROUGH THE FOREST OF DEAN TO CINDERFORD

Newnham

Three views of the station at Newnham which stood on the line from Chepstow to Cheltenham. Here, in the early 1900s, Great Western '3521' class 4-4-0 No 3546 departs with a down stopping service. No 3546 was built in 1888 as an 0-4-2ST, converted to an 0-4-4T in 1890 and converted again, to a 4-4-0 tender engine in 1900. The condition of the engine suggests that the picture was taken soon after its final conversion.

The second picture shows Newnham soon after the addition of a bay platform which was constructed for Cinderford branch services, and opened on 4 August 1907. At the same time, the existing platforms were extended. Standing in the new bay with a service to Cinderford is '517' class 0-4-2T No 564. Newnham was closed to passenger traffic on 2 November 1964.

Looking down from the road bridge on 5 June 2001, no trace of the station now remains, but behind the foliage on the right, the foundations of the goods shed can still be seen. *GW Trust/Author*

Minety & Ashton Keynes

'Castle' class 4-6-0 No 7000 *Viscount Portal* heads through Minety & Ashton Keynes with a down service to Cheltenham and Gloucester in October 1962. The station, which stood on the Swindon to Gloucester line, was opened on 31 May 1841 and was closed to passengers on 2 November 1964.

The up platform has now gone, but part of the bay platform on the left is still in situ, and this is where I stood to take this shot to show the remains of the down platform on 29 April 2001.
GW Trust/Author

Chalford

For many years, the Great Western operated steam railmotor and later auto-train services between Gloucester and Chalford. On 30 April 1960, '1400' class 0-4-2T No 1424 prepares to depart from Chalford with the 1.56pm auto-service to Gloucester. Chalford, together with many of the intermediate stations on the route, was closed on 2 November 1964.

Tetbury

The 6.10pm branch service to Kemble hauled by '5800' class 0-4-2T No 5800 waits at Tetbury on 21 July 1954. The branch was opened by the Great Western on 2 December 1889. Originally a timber station, it was replaced by a standard red brick entrance building in 1916. Tetbury was closed to passenger traffic on 6 April 1964.

The station entrance road and gates are still in evidence, as is the goods shed. The goods yard now forms the town car park. Seen from approximately the same spot on 28 June 2001, new houses occupy part of the yard.
GW Trust/Author

On 16 September 2001, the 09.35 First Great Western HST service from Cheltenham to Paddington passes the site of Chalford station on its climb up to Sapperton Tunnel. Part of the up platform can still be seen. However, the station entrance is now a builder's yard.
GW Trust/Author

St Mary's Crossing Halt

St Mary's Crossing Halt was situated
on the Swindon to Gloucester line
between Chalford and Brimscombe.
Opened by the Great Western on
12 October 1903, it was closed on
2 November 1964. Taken from the
down platform, '1400' class 0-4-2T
No 1409 arrives with the auto-service
from Gloucester to Chalford.

Seen from approximately the same
spot on 5 June 2001, the crossing box is
still open but all trace of the halt is now
gone. In the distance is Class 158
No 158784 on a Swindon to Gloucester
service. *GW Trust/Author*

Brimscombe Shed

Brimscombe engine shed was opened in around 1845 and housed banking engines to assist trains on the climb up to Sapperton. The single-road shed was officially closed on 28 October 1963, but continued as a servicing point for several months after this date. On 7 March 1964, '5101' class 2-6-2T No 4109 takes water during a break between banking duties. The station, seen in the background, was closed to passengers on 2 November 1964.

Part of the shed wall still survives, as seen in this picture taken on 18 July 2001. *Hugh Ballantyne/Author*

Cheltenham Spa (Malvern Road)

Cheltenham Spa (Malvern Road) station, pictured here in the early 1960s, was opened on 3 March 1908. It comprised an island platform linked to the entrance road by a footbridge. The station was closed to passengers on 3 January 1966.

The trackbed is now a footpath, but the brick abutment of the footbridge could still be seen on the left on 16 September 2001. *GW Trust/Author*

Cheltenham (Malvern Road) Shed

The old Great Western engine shed at Cheltenham (Malvern Road) is seen here in October 1950. Standing outside the shed is '4300' class 2-6-0 No 5336, diesel railcar No W25W and a '4575' class 2-6-2T. The shed was opened by the Great Western in 1907 and closed on 1 October 1963.

Today, the shed buildings have been converted to warehouses for Travis-Perkins, builders' merchants. The two buildings can be seen in this picture taken on 16 September 2001. Interestingly, the entrance to the yard is through a pair of original Great Western gates. *GW Trust/Author*

Cheltenham St James's

The imposing entrance to the Great Western station at Cheltenham St James's, which was opened on 23 October 1847. It was served by trains from Birmingham via Stratford-on-Avon, and by M&SWJR trains from Andover. The station was closed to passengers on 3 January 1966 and the area has been redeveloped in recent years. St James's House office block has been built and is seen here on 16 September 2001, the building on the right providing a reference point. *GW Trust/Author*

Toddington

Toddington station, on the Cheltenham to Stratford-on-Avon 'Honeybourne' line was opened on 1 December 1904 and is seen here on 27 February 1960 as '5700' class 0-6-0PT No 9727 arrives with the 1pm local stopping service from Cheltenham St James's to Broadway.

It is now the headquarters of the Gloucestershire Warwickshire Railway which I visited on 29 July 2001 and took this shot of the restored station from an adjacent train. *Hugh Ballantyne/Author*

Stratford-on-Avon

A view of Stratford-on-Avon in Great Western days. The station at this time comprised two main platforms and a through bay. The branch from Hatton to Stratford was opened on 10 October 1860 and that from Honeybourne to Stratford in July 1859, the two lines being connected on 24 July 1861. Passenger services commenced over the North Warwick line between Stratford and Tyseley on 1 July 1908. The closure of the Honeybourne and Cheltenham line to passengers on 7 March 1960, and to goods on 2 January 1967, made Stratford a terminus station once again.

Winchcombe

Winchcombe station is pictured here on 11 June 1949. The section from Winchcombe to Toddington was opened on 1 February 1905, and from Winchcombe to Bishops Cleeve on 1 June 1906. Passenger services were withdrawn from Winchcombe on 7 March 1960 and after goods services were withdrawn on 2 November 1964 the track was removed and the site cleared.

About 6½ miles of the route south of Toddington has now been relaid by the Gloucestershire Warwickshire Railway and Winchcombe has been completely restored with new platforms. The 'new' station building here was salvaged from Monmouth Troy and has been rebuilt using mainly volunteer labour, as seen here on 16 September 2001. The whole line is a great credit to the many volunteer helpers. *GW Trust/Author*

On Sunday, 29 July 2001, Class 150 No 150019 arrives on a special working from Leamington, the usual service from Birmingham having failed. The main station building is still in use but passenger facilities on the island platform now comprise a small bus type shelter.
GW Trust/Author

Leamington Spa

The 9.10am service from Paddington to Birkenhead prepares to depart from Leamington Spa on 1 April 1961 hauled by '6100' class 2-6-2T No 6116. The usual 'King' had failed and apparently the Prairie tank took the 13-coach train onwards to Birmingham unaided except for a banking engine at Hatton.

Class 168 No 168112 arrives with a Birmingham to Marylebone service on 26 July 2001. The up platform and north bay were extended in the 1970s.
GW Trust/Author

Old Hill

'6400' class 0-6-0PT No 6418 with push-pull trailer No 160 arrives at Old Hill from Stourbridge Junction on 19 August 1961 to work the service to Dudley. The Dudley branch can be seen curving away to the right, the route being known locally as the 'Bumble Hole line', named after the local area. The platform on the left was part of a triangle and once served the Halesowen branch. Passenger services from Old Hill to Dudley were withdrawn on 14 June 1964. The branch survived for goods traffic until 1 January 1968, being lifted in May of the same year.

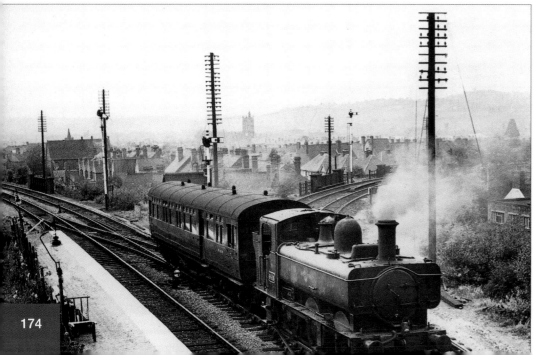

Birmingham Snow Hill

'Star' class 4-6-0 No 4058 *Princess Augusta* brings an up service into Birmingham Snow Hill on 4 September 1934. Notice the motley collection of stock which includes a mail coach. The station was closed on 6 March 1972, but a new station was opened on the same site on 2 October 1987. Since then, the line has been extended through to Handsworth and Smethwick Junction.

Looking from approximately the same spot on 26 July 2001, Class 168 No 168002 is being cleaned in preparation for its departure to Marylebone. The Midland Metro tram system, which opened on 31 May 1999, runs between Birmingham Snow Hill and Wolverhampton and terminates at the platform on the right. *GW Trust/Author*

On 26 July 2001, Class 150 No 150011 arrives at Old Hill with a Central Trains Malvern to Birmingham Snow Hill service. The junction has now gone and the trackbed is overgrown. *G. D. King/Author*

Hartlebury

A down goods service hauled by '2800' class 2-8-0 No 2833 passes through Hartlebury on 5 September 1958. This was the junction station for the Severn Valley line to Stourport and Bewdley and is still open, served by Central Trains services from Birmingham Snow Hill and Worcester.

Class 150 No 150016 calls with a Central Trains service from Malvern to Birmingham Snow Hill on a wet 5 June 2001. The main station building has been extended and is now in private use. *GW Trust/Author*

Stourport-on-Severn

A pair of diesel railcars: No W32W with the 5.30pm service from Hartlebury to Bewdley, and No W36W with the 5.33pm service from Bewdley to Hartlebury, pass at Stourport-on-Severn on 5 September 1958. Passenger services over the Hartlebury to Bewdley branch were withdrawn on 5 January 1970.

It is difficult to imagine that there once was a railway here. This housing estate now covers the site of Stourport station, as seen on 5 June 2001.
GW Trust/Author

Cleobury Mortimer

Diesel railcar No W26W calls at Cleobury Mortimer on 5 September 1958 with the 4.58pm service from Tenbury Wells to Bewdley. Passenger services were withdrawn over the branch on 1 August 1962. The wagons on the left are standing on the goods-only Cleobury Mortimer & Ditton Priors Railway, which was closed on 16 April 1965.

A plantation of conifers now precludes a photograph being taken from the same location so I have included this view looking in the other direction. Part of the platform is still in situ, as is the station building which is now used as a holiday home; 5 June 2001.
GW Trust/Author

Tenbury Wells

The 4.10pm service from Kidderminster formed by diesel railcar No W26W is seen here at Tenbury Wells on 5 September 1958. Passenger services from Bewdley to Woofferton Junction were withdrawn on 1 August 1962.

For many years the site of the station was covered by a water bottling plant but this has recently been removed allowing this picture, taken on 5 June 2001. The building on the right is the original station and part of the platform can still be seen. The road bridge and house also provide reference points. *GW Trust/Author*

Arley

Two members of the station staff pose for the photographer in this early view of Arley station on the Severn Valley Railway.

As can be seen, the period nature of the station has been well preserved by the present-day Severn Valley Railway in this picture taken on 18 July 2001. *GW Trust/Author*

Bridgnorth

An ex-Great Western diesel railcar is unloaded at Bridgnorth in August 1960 after arriving with the service from Hartlebury. Passenger services between Shrewsbury and Bewdley were withdrawn on 7 September 1963. Since 23 May 1970 the southern section of the branch from Bridgnorth has been operated by the Severn Valley Railway.

The station area at Bridgnorth shows little change but the goods yard now accommodates the locomotive shed and sidings. The goods shed has been incorporated into the locomotive works; 5 June 2001.

Craven Arms

Craven Arms was the junction station for the Great Western's Newport to Shrewsbury line, the ex-LNWR Central Wales line from Swansea and the Great Western branch to Much Wenlock. Here, in September 1945, un-named 'Modified Hall' No 6961 (later *Stedham Hall*) waits with a through service from South Wales.

Much Wenlock

Much Wenlock was situated on the branch from Buildwas Junction to Craven Arms. Opened from Buildwas to Much Wenlock by the Much Wenlock & Severn Junction Railway on 1 February 1862, it was extended through to Craven Arms on 16 December 1867. The fine station at Much Wenlock is pictured here in August 1959 with '5700' class 0-6-0PT No 3744 on a service to Wellington (Salop). Passenger services between Much Wenlock and Craven Arms were withdrawn in 1951, and to Wellington on 23 July 1962.

The station building is still very much intact; owned by the local council, it has now been converted into four residences. The platform face is still visible and forms part of the gardens; 5 June 2001. *Dr G. Smith/Author*

As already mentioned, the branch to Much Wenlock was closed in 1951, but the other two routes are still open. The station has been altered somewhat, with little in the way of passenger comforts, and is seen here on 20 July 2001 as Class 158 No 158837 arrives with the 11.18 Wales & West Alphaline service from Bristol Temple Meads to Manchester Piccadilly.
GW Trust/David Heath

Wellington (Salop) Shed

A view of Wellington engine shed yard in GW days. On the right is '5101' class 2-6-2T No 5129 and on the left GWR 2-4-0 No 3223. The engine shed was opened by the Great Western in 1876 and closed in August 1964.

On 25 June 2001, the up loop platform is closed and fenced off and part of the old shed yard is used to store contractors' containers. The whole area is now overgrown. *GW Trust/D. Burns*

Market Drayton

Market Drayton was the main intermediate station on the Wellington to Crewe line. The line was closed to passenger traffic on 9 September 1963, and to goods traffic on 1 May 1967. In this late 1950s view 'Grange' class 4-6-0 No 6823 *Oakley Grange* passes through with a down goods service.

As seen from the road overbridge on 25 June 2001, the station site has been covered by a rather untidy industrial development. *R. H. G. Simpson/D. Burns*

Ellesmere

Ellesmere was situated on the Cambrian branch from Oswestry to Whitchurch and was served by trains from Wrexham to Ellesmere.

In September 1962, the last week of operation, '1400' class 0-4-2T No 1432 waits to depart with the auto-train service to Wrexham Central. The Wrexham to Ellesmere branch was closed to passengers on 10 September 1962, while the Oswestry to Whitchurch line remained open for passenger traffic until 18 January 1965.

The road bridge is the reference point in this picture taken on 25 June 2001. The station site is now a scrapyard and (below left) the station building, which is grade 2 listed, is now used by an engineering firm.
G. Marsh/D. Burns

Hooton

The Great Western in the Wirral with
'3500' class 2-4-0T No 1495 on the
Hooton to Helsby railmotor service
*c*1920s. The service operated over the
8¹/₂-mile branch, and connected Hooton
on the GWR Birkenhead to Chester line
with Helsby on the LMS, Chester and
Warrington line.

Today, the service in the Wirral has
been electrified and is operated by
Arriva Merseyside. On 13 September
2001, Class 507 EMU No 507030
arrives at Hooton with the 11.19 service
to Ellesmere Port. *GW Trust/D. Burns*

Section 5 - Wales

Prior to the Grouping in 1923, railway services in Wales were being operated by no fewer than 17 different railway companies. Today this once vast rail system has been reduced to just a few lines.

It seems that over the years the Principality has had rather more than its fair share of closures. Many of these in South Wales are of course due to the rundown of the coal mining industry from literally hundreds of collieries (in 1913 there were about 600 rail-connected collieries) to, at the time of writing, just the lone survivor, Tower Colliery, near Hirwaun.

In South Wales, main line services continue to be operated by First Great Western HSTs with secondary services operated by Wales & Borders using Class 150, 153, 156 and 158 DMUs. Wales & Borders is a new franchise and was inaugurated on 14 October 2001. In recent years, new stations have been opened under the joint funding Swanline initiative, at Briton Ferry, Skewen, and Pyle.

The South Wales valley line services to Maesteg, Treherbert, Merthyr, Rhymney and Aberdare are operated by Valley Lines, a trading name of the Cardiff Railway Company. Many of these services run through to Penarth and Barry Island and are operated using Class 142 and 143 units. In recent years, some peak hour services have been run using hired-in locomotives and coaching stock.

Another survivor is the ex-LNWR Central Wales line from Llandeilo to Craven Arms. Today, the service, which is operated by Wales & Borders, comprises four trains daily in each direction.

In North Wales, the ex-Cambrian Railways route to Aberystwyth and Pwllheli is still open and is operated by Wales & Borders with Class 150, 156 and 158 units. During the summer, through services from Birmingham to Pwllheli and Aberystwyth are operated by Central Trains. To cut costs, since 1988, the ex-Cambrian route has been converted to radio signalling, controlled from the Machynlleth Signalling Centre.

There is still a considerable amount of freight, particularly in South Wales with coal, oil and steel being prominent. A number of old passenger branches remain open, mainly for coal traffic. EWS, which operates the services, has once again introduced mixed freights. The bulk of these services now use Class 56, 60 and 66 diesels. The once prolific Class 37s have now become a rarity in the area.

Cardiff Canton is the major servicing point for EWS locomotives in South Wales and Wales & Borders has established its own servicing depot on the site of the old Great Western carriage sheds at Canton. Stabling facilities for locomotives are also provided at Margam, Newport and Landore.

Steam enthusiasts are well catered for in Wales, with the occasional steam runs over some of the valley lines. Standard gauge railways have been established by the Swansea Vale Railway at Upper Bank, the Pontypool & Blaenavon Railway at Blaenavon, the Vale of Glamorgan at Barry and the Gwili Railway, which operates between Bronwydd Arms and Danycoed. The Llanelli & Mynydd Mawr Railway proposes to establish a standard gauge museum on the site of Cynheidre Colliery.

In the north, the Llangollen Railway operates steam trains between Llangollen and Carrog. North Wales is famous for its many narrow gauge railways, but in South Wales, narrow gauge operations have also been established, by the Brecon Mountain Railway and the Teifi Valley Railway.

Chepstow Bridge

Brunel's bridge over the River Wye at Chepstow is pictured here on 15 August 1960. It was partially opened on 19 July 1852 and fully opened, with double tracks, on 18 April 1853. The main supporting chains of the suspension bridge were carried in the two cast-iron cylinders. In 1962 the bridge was rebuilt, with modern steel trusses replacing the old cast-iron tubular structure.

The 'new' bridge is pictured here on 13 September 2001. Behind the rail bridge is a modern road bridge built to take the main Chepstow to Gloucester road (A48) over the river.
GW Trust/Author

Chepstow

Chepstow station is seen here on 10 June 1956 with '5700' class 0-6-0PT No 7787 arriving with the 10.40am service to Monmouth Troy. Station West signalbox was closed on 20 February 1955.

The station, which is now an unmanned halt, is served by Wales & Border, services between Cardiff and Gloucester. This view from the down platform on 1 May 2001 shows the refurbished footbridge. The station building is in private use, as is the large ex-Great Western goods shed.
GW Trust/Author

Severn Tunnel Junction

The large station at Severn Tunnel Junction is pictured here in the early 1960s. Waiting to depart is '5101' class 2-6-2T No 4159 with a car ferry service via Severn Tunnel to Pilning (High Level). There was once a large engine shed and extensive yards, sadly now all gone.

Severn Tunnel Junction is now essentially an unstaffed halt served by Wales & Borders services between Cardiff, Bristol and Gloucester. Although the footbridge remains, all other original station buildings have been removed and replaced by a couple of modern shelters. The up relief platform is now devoid of track. On 13 September 2001, an HST powers through a deserted Severn Tunnel Junction with the 14.55 First Great Western service from Cardiff Central to Paddington. *GW Trust/Author*

New Tredegar

New Tredegar was situated on the Brecon & Merthyr branch from Rhymney Lower to Aberbargoed Junction. New Tredegar became the terminus for passenger services when the northern section of the branch to Rhymney Lower was closed due to a landslide on 14 April 1930. Here, on 27 October 1962, '5700' class 0-6-0PT No 3772 runs round its train at New Tredegar in preparation for its return trip to Bedwas and Newport.

Newport Cardiff Road Sidings

Cardiff Road Newport is shown here on 31 January 1930 from Courtybella crossing. The Cardiff Road sidings were originally part of the Sirhowy Tramroad which ran from Park Junction via Maesglas to Newport Dock Street. After closure in 1880s the line was used for storage sidings which were removed just before World War 2, with part of the trackbed being used to widen the A48 road and to provide a slip road.

On 13 September 2001, all sign of the railway has gone. The houses continue to provide a reference point. Behind the photographer it is still possible to see where the lines entered the docks. The building on the left is the Royal Gwent Hospital. *GW Trust/Author*

The branch was closed to passengers on 31 December 1962 and when I visited the site on 13 September 2001 only part of the up platform remained to remind us that there once was a railway here. *GW Trust/Author*

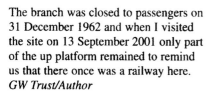

189

Groeswen Halt

Groeswen Halt stood on the Caerphilly to Pontypridd branch. This section of the branch was opened for passengers by the Alexandra, Newport & South Wales Docks Railway on 28 December 1887. The rail-level halt was opened for steam railmotor services which were introduced on the branch during 1904. The halt is seen here, possibly soon after opening. The small ADR signalbox controlled the sidings to the nearby colliery. The house on the top right was built for the colliery manager.

The second picture shows the halt just two days before closure on 15 September 1956. The signalbox has gone, and one wonders if anyone used the halt at this time.

I visited the site on 1 May 2001, and the trackbed is now a footpath, but the stone base of the signalbox can still be seen. *GW Trust/Author*

Senghenydd

The 12½-mile Aber Valley branch from Caerphilly started life as a mineral line. It was extended to Senghenydd by the Rhymney Railway and opened for passenger and goods traffic on 1 February 1894. The terminus station at Senghenydd is seen here in this early postcard view, c1920s, which also shows the colliery. Passenger services were withdrawn on 15 June 1964, goods traffic having been withdrawn some two years earlier, on 2 July 1962. The line remained in use until 1977 to serve the nearby Windsor Colliery.

Looking down from the roadbridge over what was the old trackbed on 13 September 2001 shows the site covered with housing. The main reference point between the two pictures is the 1904 ex-County Police Station, seen here on the right. *GW Trust/Author*

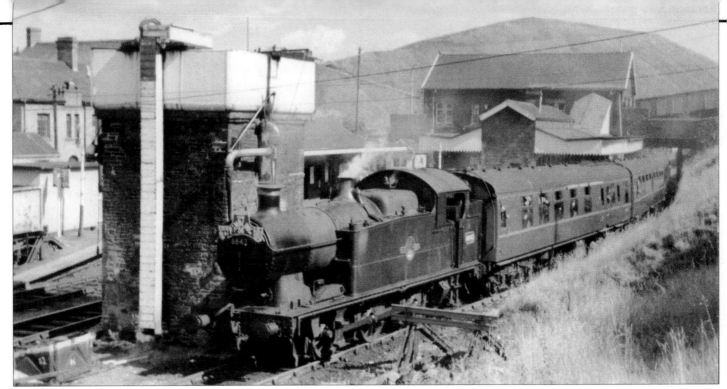

Bargoed

The 'Rambling 56', an enthusiasts' special commemorating the end of the ex-Great Western '5600' class 0-6-2Ts, hauled by No 6643, calls at the old Rhymney Railway station at Bargoed on Saturday, 31 July 1965.

On 13 September 2001, the station has been completely modernised with new buildings and a footbridge which has been provided with lifts for the disabled. The down bay platform has gone, as has the water tower. The large signalbox was moved from Cymmer Afan to Bargoed and was opened on 9 November 1970. At the same time, the line from Bargoed to Rhymney was singled. *GW Trust/Author*

Rhymney Shed

The engine shed at Rhymney, which stood adjacent to the station, is pictured here in the 1950s. On the right are '5600' class 0-6-2Ts Nos 5622 and 6655. The three-road shed was built by the Rhymney Railway in around 1864 and was closed in March 1965.

Nothing remained of the shed on 13 September 2001. The station is on the right and the track on the left connects with some stabling sidings. However, the buffer stop and siding that were in front of the signalbox are still in situ and provide a reference point. *R. E. Toop/Author*

Rhymney

A view of the Rhymney Railway station at Rhymney looking south c1910. On the right is the engine shed and on the left the station entrance and ticket office. From Rhymney, services continued northwards over the former Rhymney and LNWR joint line to Rhymney Bridge and Nantybwch which was closed on 23 September 1953.

Today, the line terminates here and Valley Line trains operate between Rhymney, Cardiff and Penarth. The much-reduced station is seen here on 13 September 2001. Only one platform is now in use, but the original Rhymney Railway station building survives.
GW Trust/Author

Nelson & Llancaiach

The former Vale of Neath station at Nelson & Llancaiach depicted here on 28 December 1963 was the junction station for the Taff-Bargoed branch to Dowlais. At the bay platform is '5600' class 0-6-2T No 6612 with the 12.37pm service from Ystrad Mynach to Dowlais Cae Harris. Passenger services over the Vale of Neath and the Taff-Bargoed lines were withdrawn on 15 June 1964 and the station was closed.

Although the platform on the left is now fenced off and the same view is not possible, both Vale of Neath platforms survive, as can be seen in this photograph taken on 13 September 2001. The line is still in operation serving Cwmbargoed opencast site. *Hugh Ballantyne/ Author*

Bedlinog

Bedlinog, pictured here *c*1910, stood on the Taff-Bargoed line to Dowlais Cae Harris. The station, as with many others in Wales, served the local mining community. It was closed to passengers on 15 June 1964.

The single line is still operational as far as Cwmbargoed opencast site, and part of the platform can still be seen, as can later concrete steps from the road above; 13 September 2001.
GW Trust/Author

Dowlais Cae Harris

The Taff-Bargoed branch terminated at Dowlais Cae Harris (formerly Lloyd Street). The station comprised an island platform, and is seen here on 1 June 1962 as '5600' class 0-6-2T No 5662 prepares to depart with a service to Ystrad Mynach.

The station was closed on 15 June 1964 and was demolished in 1970. New housing is gradually spreading across the site of the railway and the main reference point is the large white building seen in both pictures; 13 September 2001. *GW Trust/Author*

Quaker's Yard High Level

Class 5101 2-6-2T No 5103 arrives at Quaker's Yard High Level on 5 September 1959 with the 11.19am service from Neath to Pontypool Road. On the right, diverging away, is the ex-Rymney Railway Quaker's Yard to Merthyr line which closed to passengers in 1951. High Level signalbox was closed on 15 June 1964, the same day as the station.

Dowlais Top

'5600' class 0-6-2T No 5670 departs from Dowlais Top on 5 September 1959 with the 12.45 (SO) service to Cardiff Queen Street. The ex-Brecon & Merthyr station, which stands 1,250ft above sea level, can be seen on the left. It was opened to passengers on 1 September 1868 and closed to passengers on 31 December 1962.

The trackbed down to Rhymney Bridge has now been swallowed up by the A465 Heads of the Valleys road to Abergavenny. The station building survives and has been converted into offices. The land in the foreground is private and fenced, hence the slightly different angle; 13 September 2001. *Hugh Ballantyne/Author*

The trackbed now forms a road into a housing estate and the slag heap on the horizon has been landscaped. Quaker's Yard Low Level, which is still open, is on the lower left of the picture; 1 May 2001. *GW Trust/Author*

Mountain Ash (Oxford Street)

An early postcard view of the Taff Vale station at Mountain Ash (Oxford Street). Passenger services were withdrawn on 16 March 1964 but were reinstated on 3 October 1988 to a new station which was opened on the same day. This station has now been closed and replaced by another new station just south of the 1988 platform.

This view, taken on 20 February 2001, shows the now-closed 1988 platform. The track has been realigned and the new station, which was opened on 29 January 2001, is on the right and just behind the photographer. GW Trust/Author

Mountain Ash (Cardiff Road)

Standing on the other side of the River Cynon was the Great Western station at Mountain Ash (Cardiff Road). This station can just be seen on the right as '5600' class 0-6-2T No 5633 passes through on 12 January 1960 with a westbound goods service. Mountain Ash (Cardiff Road) was closed to passengers on 15 June 1964.

Looking from the adjacent roadbridge on 20 February 2001, flood control measures have widened the river at this point, encroaching on what was the trackbed. The 'Allen's Arms Hotel' has gone but the old chapel provides a good reference point. *S. Rickard/Author*

Aberdare High Level

An early but undated view of the Vale of Neath Railway station at Aberdare High Level where the platforms were staggered. The goods shed was wooden and the 1867 locomotive depot is just out of view on the left. The station was closed to passengers on 15 June 1964, but the line remained open for coal traffic as far as Tower Colliery (Hirwaun).

The branch to Aberdare was reopened for passenger traffic once again on 3 October 1988. The remains of the old station were empty and unused on 20 February 2001. The 1988 platform can be seen in the distance, with a Class 142 DMU waiting to leave with a service to Cardiff and Barry Island. *GW Trust/Author*

Aberdare Low Level

Aberdare Low Level station in 1956. It was served by trains from Cardiff Queen Street, Pontypridd, Abercynon and Merthyr and closed to passengers on 16 March 1964. Since then the site has been cleared and redeveloped.

Seen from the same spot on 20 February 2001, part of the old station area is now a bus station. The bollards in the foreground mark the site of the street on the right in the first photograph.
G. Davies/Author

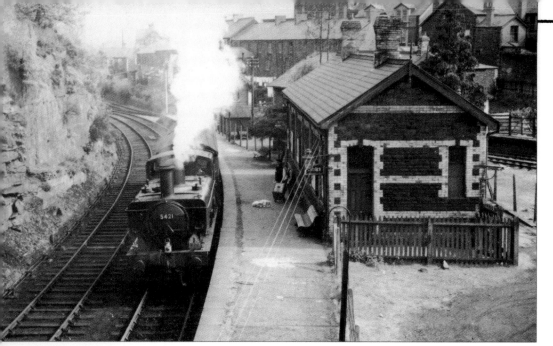

Ynysybwl

The Ynysybwl branch was opened by the Taff Vale Railway in 1886 to serve the nearby Lady Windsor Colliery. Passenger services commenced on 1 January 1890 and were withdrawn on 28 July 1952 with goods traffic being withdrawn during November 1959. The branch remained open as far as Lady Windsor Colliery, with services over the branch ceasing with the closure of the colliery in March 1988. Ynysybwl station is seen here on 13 May 1952 with '5400' class 0-6-0PT No 5421 in charge of the service from Pontypridd.

In recent years, the station building has been restored and extended, and is now in commercial use, as seen on 20 February 2001. *R. C. Riley/Author*

Porth

Looking south from the station footbridge at Porth on 29 September 1962, as '5101' class 2-6-2T No 4160 arrives with a service from Barry Island to Treherbert. Porth was the junction station for the Taff Vale branches to Maerdy and Treherbert. The Maerdy branch is now closed but the Treherbert line is still open.

A Class 143 DMU is seen departing with a service from Treherbert to Penarth on 20 February 2001. The old footbridge is still in situ, but I could not use it as my vantage point since it is deemed unsafe and fenced off.
GW Trust/Author

Tylorstown

Tylorstown on the Taff Vale Maerdy branch, *c*1920s. The tank engine in the background is leaving the Ferndale Colliery sidings. This station was closed on 15 June 1964.

Photographed on 20 February 2001, the site looks a mess. The remains of the up platform can be seen on the right, and a large concrete structure, now unused, covers the old station entrance.
GW Trust/Author

Ferndale

The Taff Vale station at Ferndale, on the branch to Maerdy, in June 1922. The station served the local mining community, with to the north, the upper, middle and lower Fan pits and to the south, Ferndale pits. The station was closed on 15 June 1964.

On 20 February 2001, part of the up platform (right) and cattle dock (left) could still be seen. *GW Trust/Author*

Ferndale Shed

The engine shed at Ferndale stood just to the north of the station and is seen here on 22 September 1957. It was opened by the Taff Vale Railway in 1884, originally as a four-road shed, but was reduced to two roads in the early 1930s. A sub-shed of Treherbert, it closed in September 1964.

Today, the adjacent coal pits are gone and the whole area has been landscaped, but it is still possible to see where the shed once stood. An original Taff Vale gate is still in situ at the end of a short footpath that once led to the shed; 20 February 2001. *A. Gould/Author*

Maerdy

The terminus of the branch at Maerdy.
Standing at the single platform on
6 November 1957 is '4575' class
2-6-2T No 5574 with auto-trailers
Nos W1709W and W254W forming the
12.25pm service to Porth. The sidings
in the background served the nearby
Maerdy Colliery. The building on the
right housed the branch auto-cars.

The branch was closed on 15 June
1964, and since then all trace of the
station has disappeared under a new
road, part of which still forms a
reference point; 20 February 2001.
Hugh Ballantyne/Author

Treorchy

An early postcard view of the Taff Vale
station at Treorchy. Passing with an up
goods service is a Taff Vale 'K' class
0-6-0. The up platform was taken out of
use when the line was singled between
Cwmparc signalbox and Treherbert on
25-27 November 1972.

The down side buildings were
removed in 1972 and replaced with the
bus shelter, seen here on 20 February
2001 as Class 142 No 142086 departs
with the 11.31 Valley Lines service to
Barry Island. The large warehouse on
the right is still in use. *GW Trust/Author*

Llwynypia

Some lads pose for the photographer on the attractive footbridge at Llwynypia. The picture is undated but was probably taken around the turn of the last century. Llwynypia is situated on the Taff Vale branch from Pontypridd to Treherbert, which was opened on 7 August 1856.

I visited the station on 20 February 2001 and took my shot from the adjacent road overbridge of Class 143 No 143609 on a Treherbert to Barry Island service. The up platform has seen some refurbishment, and a concrete footbridge has replaced the cast-iron bridge. Llwynypia was converted to a park-and-ride station during 1989.
GW Trust/Author

Treherbert Shed

The ex-Great Western engine shed at Treherbert is pictured on 9 October 1931, soon after opening. The shed replaced an earlier Taff Vale depot that stood nearby. On view are a number of '5600' class 0-6-2Ts including Nos 5636, 5662 and 5680.

Treherbert was closed on 1 March 1965 and since then the site has been covered by industrial development as seen here on 20 February 2001. *GW Trust/Author*

Merthyr

This photograph shows the terminus at Merthyr in August 1951. On the left, '5600' class 0-6-2T No 5691 runs round its train, whilst on the right '6400' class 0-6-0PTs Nos 6434 and 6427 wait to depart with auto-services to Dowlais and Pontsticill Junction. During 1971, the main station buildings were demolished and the station reduced to a single platform.

Treherbert

Seen from the footbridge over the level crossing, '5600' class 0-6-2T No 5627 shunts some empty stock at Treherbert in November 1961, having arrived earlier with a service from Penarth. The original TVR platform can be seen on the left. It was removed in 1979.

The footbridge has now gone and the crossing has been downgraded in this rail-level view taken on 20 February 2001. On the right are the stabling sidings. Class 150 No 150280 stands at the single platform which has replaced the earlier station. The original TVR engine shed was situated on the right. *GW Trust/Author*

Since I visited the site in 1993 further changes have taken place. The station area has now been converted to a car park, the new platform and ticket office being opened on 14 January 1996, as seen on my visit of 13 September 2001. *GW Trust/Author*

Cefn Coed

Cefn Coed was situated on the Brecon to Merthyr line and just north of the 253yd-long Cefn Viaduct. Pictured here in November 1961, shortly before closure to passenger traffic, is a '6400' class 0-6-0PT on an auto-train service from Pontsticill Junction to Merthyr. The station was closed to passengers on 13 November 1961 and to goods traffic on 4 May 1964.

Nothing remains of the station today and modern flats now occupy the area. However, the Station Hotel is still open. In this view taken on 13 September 2001, I have widened the scene to include part of Cefn Viaduct, a listed structure, and now used as a footpath and cycle track. *GW Trust/Author*

Llwydcoed

Llwydcoed station, pictured here on 23 July 1962, has a service arriving from Merthyr behind '6400' class 0-6-0PT No 6433. The 7½-mile branch from Merthyr to Hirwaun was opened by the Vale of Neath Railway on 2 November 1853 and closed to passengers and goods on 31 December 1962.

Pontsticill Junction

'2251' class 0-6-0 No 2247 arrives at Pontsticill Junction in July 1961 with a service from Newport to Brecon. On the right, a '5700' class 0-6-0PT stands in the Merthyr branch platform. Passenger services from Pontsticill Junction to Merthyr were withdrawn on 13 November 1961 and from Newport to Brecon on 31 December 1962.

The site of the junction is now used by the narrow gauge Brecon Mountain Railway which was opened on 8 June 1980. On a very dull 13 September 2001, the narrow gauge line can be seen on the right. The signalbox is still standing, and the old station building has been refurbished to provide bed and breakfast accommodation.
GW Trust/Author

Seen from the cutting on 20 February 2001, the trackbed is now a footpath and apart from the road overbridge, nothing remains. *G. Davies/Author*

211

Abernant

The only other intermediate station on the Hirwaun branch was at Abernant, seen here on 23 July 1962 with 0-6-0PT No 6433. This station was opened in November 1854, and closed on 31 December 1962. The poster on the right advertises off-peak trips to Swansea for 6s 9d.

Here, the platform survives, and as with Llwydcoed, the trackbed has been turned into a footpath and cycleway; 20 February 2001. *G. Davies/Author*

Duffryn Yard shed

Duffryn Yard shed stood alongside the Port Talbot to Maesteg line. It was opened in 1896 by the Port Talbot Railway and supplied goods engines for the industrial area of Port Talbot. The depot, seen here on 1 June 1926, was rebuilt by the Great Western in 1931 and eventually closed by British Railways on 2 March 1964.

On 3 September 2001, the site is seen covered with a housing estate. The concrete flyover of the M4 motorway crosses the valley at this point. The two rows of railway cottages can still be seen amongst the 1960s housing. *GW Trust/Author*

Pyle

The 3.25pm (SO) auto-train from Pyle to Porthcawl hauled by '6400' class 0-6-0PT No 6431 stands at Pyle on 7 July 1962. The Porthcawl branch was closed to passengers on 9 September 1963 and Pyle station was closed on 2 November 1964.

As part of the Swanline initiative a new station at Pyle, situated about half a mile to the west of the old station, was opened on 11 July 1994. It is pictured here, devoid of passengers, on 3 September 2001. *S. Rickard/Author*

Bridgend

Bridgend was the junction station services to Cymmer, Abergwynfi, Treherbert and Barry. Seen from the station footbridge on 27 October 1962, '7200' class 2-8-2T No 7206 passes through with a down mixed goods service for Swansea. On the left, standing in the bay is a train for Maesteg. Passenger services between Bridgend and Maesteg were withdrawn on 15 July 1970.

Porthcawl

This view shows the terminus station at Porthcawl on 9 June 1960. The passenger station, at one time the destination for many excursion trains, was opened on 1 August 1865. The line on the left once served the harbour coal tip sidings. As already mentioned, passenger services from Pyle were withdrawn on 9 September 1963, but goods services survived until 1 February 1965.

The road overbridge has now gone and a main road to the sea front has been constructed on what was the trackbed. The goods yard is now a car park and the old harbour sidings an open space. Some of the buildings seen in the first picture can still be identified today; 1 May 2001. *GW Trust/Author*

Seen from the same spot on 13 September 2001, a First Great Western HST arrives with a Paddington to Swansea service. The Maesteg platform has now been filled in and planted with shrubs and trees. The bay line on the right has been shortened and is currently used to stable track-testing vehicles. *GW Trust/Author*

Tondu Junction

An early, undated view of the Bridgend and Abergwynfi line platforms at Tondu Junction. The station once had four platforms serving the Ogmore Vale extension line, the Blackmill branch and the Bridgend and Abergwynfi lines.

Class 143 No 143619 arrives with a service from Maesteg to Cardiff Central on 1 May 2001. Today, only one platform survives, the northern end has been refurbished, but as can be seen, the rest is a mess. *GW Trust/Author*

Brynmenyn

Brynmenyn station was the junction for the lines to Blaengarw and Nantymoel. The first picture (top right) shows the station in the 1920s. The line to Blaengarw curves away to the left and the line to Nantymoel on the right. Passenger services to Blaengarw were withdrawn on 9 February 1953 and to Nantymoel on 5 May 1958.

The second picture (right) shows the closed station on 18 July 1967 when both lines were still in situ.

Picture three, (left) taken on 1 May 2001, shows the site of the station today. As can be seen, the track of the old branch to Blaengarw is still in place and has been recently ballasted. The section from Tondu to Pontycymer may be taken over by a railway preservation society. *GW Trust/Author*

Blaengarw

Blaengarw was the terminus of the five-mile-long Garw branch from Brynmenyn. The single-platform terminus is seen here in this undated view. The line on the right continued northwards for a short distance to serve a colliery; the whole valley was a prolific coal producing area. Passenger services were withdrawn on 9 February 1953.

Since the closure of the remaining pit in 1985, the whole area has been landscaped, but the houses on the left provide a reference point; 1 May 2001. *GW Trust/Author*

Nantymoel

Nantymoel was the terminus of a ten-mile line from Bridgend, and is seen here on 3 May 1958, the last day of passenger services over the branch. '4575' class 2-6-2T No 5524 stands at the single platform after arriving with the 11.55am (SO) service from Bridgend.

Silver birch trees were found growing on the platform when I visited the site on 1 May 2001. The line remained open for goods, but was closed in stages between 1988 and 1990. The trackbed is now a footpath and cycle track. New housing has been built on the right, in front of the old cottages, seen in the first view. *S. Rickard/Author*

Maesteg (Neath Road)

A pre-Grouping picture of the Port Talbot Railway station at Maesteg (Neath Road). The station, which stood on the line from Port Talbot to Pontyrhyll, was closed to passengers as early as 11 September 1933, but the line remained open for goods traffic until 31 August 1964.

Since closure, the whole area has been landscaped, the road overbridge has gone, and the station area is a now small park. Some of the houses on the left survive, and the high level row of cottages are still there, behind the trees as depicted on 1 May 2001. *GW Trust/Author*

Maesteg (Castle Street)

Maesteg (Castle Street) stood on the Bridgend to Abergwynfi line and is seen here on 26 July 1958. '5700' class 0-6-0PT No 7725 arrives with the 4.55pm service from Abergwynfi to Bridgend. Castle Street station was closed to passengers on 15 July 1970.

The old Castle Street station, on 1 May 2001, lies abandoned and overgrown behind a Somerfield supermarket. A large private house has been built on what was once the station entrance.

Officially opened on 30 October 1992, passenger services from Cardiff via Bridgend to Maesteg were reinstated by Mid and South Glamorgan county councils on 28 September 1992. A new station was constructed at Maesteg which shares its car park with the adjacent supermarket. The track beyond the new station is still in situ as far as Nantyffyllon but is currently out of use; 1 May 2001.
GW Trust/Author

Cymmer Afan

Cymmer Afan was once a major railway junction with three stations: Cymmer General on the Bridgend and Abergwynfi line, Cymmer Afan on the Rhondda & Swansea Bay line, and Cymmer Corrwyg (closed 22 September 1930) on the South Wales Mineral Railway. In January 1950, Cymmer General was amalgamated with Afan, and is seen here on 26 July 1958 as 0-6-0PT No 7725 arrives with the 3.55pm service from Abergwynfi to Bridgend. Cymmer Afan was closed to passengers on 15 July 1970.

Today, it is easy to trace the many lines that once ran through Cymmer. The old General station, which stood on the left of the picture, has now been completely removed, but the old R&SB platform remains, as does the station building which is now a pub. In the distance, part of the bridge, viaduct and Cymmer Tunnel remain; 1 May 2001. *GW Trust/Author*

Aberavon Town

The ex-Rhondda & Swansea Bay station at Aberavon Town is pictured here in May 1954. Standing at the platform with an SLS special over the route is '5700' class 0-6-0PT No 5734. The station, which opened as Aberavon, was renamed Aberavon & Port Talbot on 1 December 1891, Port Talbot in June 1895 and Aberavon Town on 1 July 1924. It was closed to passengers on 3 December 1962, and to goods on 3 August 1964.

Abergwynfi

Abergwynfi was the terminus of the Llynfi Valley service. On 26 July 1958, 0-6-0PT No 7725 stands at Abergwynfi after arriving with the 3.55pm service from Bridgend. Although a terminus for passengers, a short spur — seen here behind the signalbox — continued beyond the station to serve a colliery. Passenger services were withdrawn from the branch on 13 June 1960.

On 1 May 2001, some abutments and bridges still mark the site of the line. Part of the trackbed is now a footpath and cycle track. *GW Trust/Author*

The site of the station is now covered by a Tesco supermarket as seen on 3 September 2001. Beyond the supermarket the new Aberafan Shopping Centre stands where a level crossing used to be. *GW Trust/Author*

Neath General

'4300' class 2-6-0 No 6353 pulls into Neath General on 27 July 1958 with the 12.40pm service from Carmarthen to Cheltenham St James's. The station seen here was opened on 4 June 1877, and the platforms were extended in 1896. It was modernised during 1978 and has recently seen further refurbishment.

On 3 September 2001, Class 158 No 158838 departs with the 11.50 service to Manchester Piccadilly. *GW Trust/Author*

Neath (Riverside)

The former Neath & Brecon station at Neath (Riverside) on 29 September 1962. Standing at the platform is the 11.25am service to Brecon hauled by '5700' class 0-6-0PT No 3634. By this date, only one platform was in passenger use. Services from Neath (Riverside) to Swansea were withdrawn in 1936 and the station closed to passengers on 15 October 1962.

Seen from a new pedestrian footbridge on 3 September 2001, part of the down platform remains, as does the Neath Brecon Junction signalbox. The single line here is open through to the coal washery at Onllwyn. The bridge in the background carries the South Wales main line over the branch. Behind the trees on the right the whole area has been covered by the Neath to Swansea dual carriageway.
GW Trust/Author

Resolven

'5101' class 2-6-2T No 4108 awaits departure from Resolven on 26 July 1963 with the 10.55am service from Pontypool Road to Neath General. The station was closed on 15 June 1964.

Both platforms remain and the line is open as far as Cwmgwrach opencast site; 3 September 2001. *J. White/Author*

Glyn Neath

Glyn Neath station is seen here on 2 June 1962 as '5700' class 0-6-0PT No 3687 arrives with the 4.10pm service from Neath (R&SB) to Brecon. The station was opened by the Vale of Neath Railway on 24 September 1851 and closed to passengers on 15 June 1964. The section from Glyn Neath to Cwmgwrach was taken out of use on 19 August 1973 and the station area and yard are now covered by the A465 dual carriageway.

On 3 September 2001, the line of the hills is the only reference point between the two pictures. The A465 is on the left and part of the station area is now occupied by a McDonald's fast-food outlet. *GW Trust/Author*

Hirwaun

'5600' class 0-6-2T No 6605 pulls into Hirwaun in July 1962 with a Neath to Pontypool Road service. The station was opened on 24 September 1851 and closed to passengers on 15 June 1964. The line from Aberdare to Tower Colliery was singled on 2 October 1967.

This view, taken on 20 February 2001, shows the remains of the platforms. The branch is still open for MGR coal traffic as far as Tower Colliery. *GW Trust/Author*

Seven Sisters

Seven Sisters station on the Neath & Brecon line with '5700' class 0-6-0PT No 9783 calling with the 4.10pm service from Neath (R&SB) to Brecon on 4 September 1958. The station once served a small mining community; the mine like most others in South Wales is now closed, but the line is still open through to Onllwyn.

Parts of the platform survive, as does the footbridge, as seen on 3 September 2001. *GW Trust/Author*

Onllwyn

The 11.25am service from Neath (R&SB) to Brecon prepares to depart from Onllwyn on 29 September 1962 hauled by '5700' class 0-6-0PT No 8732. Standing alongside is fellow class member, No 3634. Passenger services were withdrawn on 15 October 1962 and the branch now terminates at Onllwyn washery, behind the photographer, and is operated using the 'one train working' system.

Part of the up platform is still in situ, as is the now empty ex-Neath & Brecon signalbox which was closed on 13 April 1969 but used as a block post until 1989; 3 September 2001.
GW Trust/Author

Briton Ferry Road

Briton Ferry Road stood on the Vale of Neath line, a few miles east of Swansea. The station is seen here, probably soon after it opened in October 1880 when it replaced an earlier station which had been closed on 1 March 1873. It was closed to passengers on 28 April 1936.

A new housing estate was being built on the site of the station on 3 September 2001. The water tower and the adjacent Tower Hotel provide the reference points. *GW Trust/Author*

Skewen

This view of Skewen station, taken soon after opening and looking east towards Neath, was possibly an official photograph. Replacing an earlier station, it was opened on 1 May 1910 and closed to passengers on 2 November 1964.

Looking from the bridge nothing of the station now remains, the site being marked by milepost 210.

Under the Swanline initiative, a new station was opened to the west of the old one on 11 July 1994. It is seen here on 3 September 2001 as a First Great Western HST passes with the 14.30 service from Swansea to Paddington. *GW Trust/Author*

Danygraig Shed

The original Rhondda & Swansea Bay Railway engine shed and carriage works at Danygraig on 16 June 1957. Standing outside the engine shed are, right to left: ex-Great Western '1101' class 0-4-0T No 1104, ex-Swansea Harbour Trust 0-4-0ST No 1145 and BR-built '1600' class 0-6-0PT No 1640. The shed, which was opened in 1896, closed to steam on 4 March 1960 and completely in March 1964.

I believe the building is now listed and in 2001 was being used by Gower Chemicals. On the day I visited the site a demonstration had just taken place against the company and the area was full of protesters and police; 3 September 2001. *GW Trust/Author*

Pontardulais Junction

Pontardulais Junction was the station for the Great Western line from Llanelli to Llandilo and the LNWR line from Swansea through to Craven Arms. On 26 July 1958, '5700' class 0-6-0PT No 7718 waits to depart with the 11.5am service from Llanelli to Brynamman West.

This single platform is all that is left of the old station. The ex-LNWR platforms have long gone, and have been replaced by an industrial site and car park. The signalbox was closed on 31 December 1967. Wales & Borders services between Swansea and Shrewsbury stop here only on request; 3 September 2001. *GW Trust/Author*

Glanamman

An undated view of Glanamman station (above right) on the Pantyffynnon to Garnant and Brynamman branch. The station was opened as Cross Keys and renamed Glanamman on 1 December 1884. The large building beyond the station is the Raven tin plate works. Glanamman was closed to passengers on 18 August 1958, and to goods on 30 January 1965.

The scene on 3 September 2001 (right): the remains of the platform are covered in foliage and the station building has long gone. The line, which is disused, continues through to Gwaun-cae-Gurwen. The level crossing has been blocked and fenced off. The one surviving feature from the first picture is the signalbox (left), which has been converted to a private residence. *GW Trust/Author*

Gwaun-cae-Gurwen

The signalbox and level crossing at Gwaun-cae-Gurwen is pictured here on 26 July 1958. This short branch, which left the Pantyffynnon to Brynamman branch at Garnant, served a colliery. Gwaun-cae-Gurwen Halt, which closed on 4 May 1926, was situated on the other side of the footbridge. The branch to Gwaun-cae-Gurwen opencast disposal site was closed in November 1987. The signalbox was converted to a ground frame on 19 July 1964, and closed completely on 29 July 1973.

Although showing little sign of use, a number of sidings are still in situ, the branch from Pantyffynnon being 'mothballed' since 1999. Beyond the crossing the whole area is now overgrown, but part of the building in the first picture survives; 3 September 2001. *GW Trust/Author*

Brynamman East

Situated on the other side of the road bridge from Brynamman West was the ex-Midland Railway station at Brynamman East, the terminus of the branch from Swansea St Thomas. I have included this view to show the close proximity of the two stations. The Great Western station is visible through the bridge, right. Brynamman East closed to passengers on 25 September 1950 but the single platform can still be seen in this view taken on 18 August 1958.

Brynamman West

'5700' class 0-6-0PT No 9743 waits at Brynamman West on 18 August 1958 with the 12.35pm service for Llanelli. Passenger services were withdrawn on 18 August 1958, but the branch remained open for goods traffic and to serve the nearby colliery until 28 September 1964.

Today, the whole station area has been in filled and is in partial use as a car park; 3 September 2001.
GW Trust/Author

This area is now used as a store for fairground equipment. I was told that the short tunnel under the road is still there but filled in with rubble from the demolished station; 3 September 2001.
GW Trust/Author

Ffairfach Halt

A local service from Pontardulais calls
at Ffairfach Halt on 4 September 1963,
hauled by '5700' class 0-6-0PT
No 9621.

The halt, which stands on the Central
Wales line, has now been refurbished
and is served by Wales & Borders
services between Swansea and
Shrewsbury. On 16 June 2001, Class
153 single-car unit No 153372 arrives
with the 08.55 service from Shrewsbury
— the 11.50am service from Ffairfach to
Swansea. *A. Muckley/Geoff Wright.*

Carmarthen Town

This excellent panoramic view of
Carmarthen Town station was taken in
August 1961. From left to right is '2251'
class 0-6-0 No 2298 on a service to
Aberystwyth, 'Grange' class 4-6-0
No 6843 *Poulton Grange* and 'Castle'
class 4-6-0 No 5027 *Farleigh Castle* with
an arrival from Paddington. In the bay
platform on the right is another '2251'
class 0-6-0, No 2216, on pilot duty. The
large building in the centre distance is the
engine shed which was opened in
February 1907. It was closed in April
1964 and the site is now in industrial use.
Services north of Carmarthen to Llandilo
and Aberystwyth were withdrawn on
22 February 1965.

Cwm Mawr

Cwm Mawr was the terminus of the Burry Port & Gwendreath Valley Railway. In this undated picture a pair of '5700' class 0-6-0PTs stand at the terminus. The single platform was on the right behind the signalbox. Passenger services were withdrawn on 21 September 1953 but the line remained open for coal traffic until 7 June 1965.

The view on 16 June 2001, with part of the platform surviving on the right, although the whole site may soon be redeveloped. The very overgrown branch now ends approximately 100yd southwest of the old station. *GW Trust/Geoff Wright*

The station has now effectively been reduced to a single platform and is seen here on 12 June 2001 as Class 158 No 158864 arrives with the 13.23 service from Milford Haven. *GW Trust/ Geoff Wright*

Pencader

Pencader station on 3 September 1958. Just arrived is the 3.47pm goods service from Newcastle Emlyn to Carmarthen, hauled by '5700' class 0-6-0PT No 9606.

The station was closed to passengers on 22 February 1965 and since that date the site has been cleared and is now in industrial use, as seen on 28 July 2001. *GW Trust/Geoff Wright*

Lampeter

Standing in the station at Lampeter on 3 September 1958 are '4300' class 2-6-0 No 5353 on the 5.40pm service from Aberystwyth to Carmarthen, and on the right, '2251' class 0-6-0 No 2217 with the 5.50pm service from Carmarthen to Aberystwyth. Although Lampeter was the junction station for the branch to Aberayron, the actual junction was just over a mile north of the station. Lampeter was closed to passengers on 22 February 1965 but the line remained open for goods until 22 September 1973.

Newcastle Emlyn

The terminus station at Newcastle Emlyn is seen here on 3 September 1958. The branch was closed to passengers on 15 September 1952 but remained open for goods until 22 September 1973. Waiting to depart with the 3.47pm service to Carmarthen Junction is 0-6-0PT No 9606.

The station site is now in use as a coal and general merchants' yard as photographed on 28 July 2001. Part of the platform survives and is part of a commercial garage car park. Buildings on the left give the reference point for the two pictures.
GW Trust/Geoff Wright

The site of the station is now covered by the Lampeter Mart, which was empty and unused on 28 July 2001 due to the foot-and-mouth epidemic. *GW Trust/ Geoff Wright*

Felin Fach

'7400' class 0-6-0PT No 7402 calls at Felin Fach on 3 September 1958 with the 9.47am Aberayron branch goods from Lampeter. Opened as Ystrad (Cardigan), the station was actually situated in the village of Ystrad Aeron, but was renamed Felin Fach on 1 January 1913. The station was closed to passengers on 12 February 1951, but the branch remained open for goods until 5 April 1965.

It is difficult to trace any part of the station today, but this caravan park and campsite stands approximately on the site of Felin Fach and was photographed on 28 July 2001.
GW Trust/Geoff Wright

Aberayron

The 9.47am goods service from Lampeter arrives at Aberayron on 3 September 1958, hauled by '7400' class 0-6-0PT No 7402. The 13½-mile long branch was closed to passengers on 12 February 1961 and to goods on 5 April 1965.

The site is now in industrial use but part of the platform could still be seen on 28 July 2001. On the left, the old carriage shed has been refurbished and is used for storage. *GW Trust/ Geoff Wright*

Strata Florida

'Manor' class 4-6-0 No 7815 *Fritwell Manor* stands at Strata Florida station on 1 June 1962 with the 5.40pm service from Aberystwyth to Carmarthen. Strata Florida, which opened on 1 September 1866, was closed to passengers on 22 February 1965.

The station was 2½ miles from Strata Florida Abbey and was actually located near the village of Ystrad Meurig. As can be seen in this picture taken on 28 July 2001, nothing remains of the station but the cutting beyond is still in evidence. The reference point is the two houses, centre left.
GW Trust/Geoff Wright

Glogue

'4500' class 2-6-2T No 4558 takes water at Glogue en route from Cardigan to Whitland in the 1950s. The station was interesting as the single platform had watering facilities at each end.

As can be seen here, part of the platform still survives in this picture taken on 2 July 2001. *R. H. G. Simpson/ Geoff Wright*

Llanglydwen

The Cardigan branch was opened by the Whitland & Cardigan Railway on 1 September 1886. Llanglydwen was the passing point on the branch and is seen here on 3 September 1958 as the 4.45pm service from Cardigan arrives behind '4500' class 2-6-2T No 4557. Standing in the platform is BR-built '1600' class 0-6-0PT No 1637 with the 6.15pm service to Cardigan.

The station building is now a private dwelling and the trackbed a coal yard — photographed on 2 July 2001.
GW Trust/Geoff Wright

Crymmych Arms

A view of Crymmych Arms on 3 September 1958. This was another passing point on the Whitland to Cardigan branch and waiting on the left is the 6.15pm service from Whitland to Cardigan hauled by No 1637. On the right, '4500' class 2-6-2T No 4519 passes with the Cardigan to Whitland goods. The Cardigan branch was closed to passengers on 10 September 1962 and to goods on 27 May 1963.

The scene today: the main station building survives as does the road overbridge, but the rest of the site is in light industrial use; 2 July 2001. *GW Trust/Geoff Wright*

Haverfordwest

An early 1960s view of Haverfordwest with '4300' class 2-6-0 No 7321 on the 3.40pm service to Neyland. Standing in the yard on the right is fellow class member, No 6316.

On 18 June 2001, Class 158 No 158834 departs with the 10.50 service to Cardiff and Bristol. The station has survived well, but the yard on the right is now in industrial use. *GW Trust/Author*

Lamphey

The single-platform station at Lamphey in an undated but early view. The station is situated on the ex-Pembroke & Tenby Railway branch and was opened with the railway on 30 July 1863.

Today, Lamphey is an unmanned halt where trains stop by request. The main station building has been demolished and replaced by a small stone shelter, but the old stationmaster's house survives as a private residence. Class 158 No 158834 arrives with the 15.27 service from Pembroke to Swansea on 18 June 2001. *GW Trust/Geoff Wright*

Neyland

The terminus station at Neyland is seen here on 4 September 1958 with '4300' class 2-6-0 No 5324 just arrived with the 8am service from Swansea High Street. Neyland was the terminus of the South Wales Railway and connected with the steamboat services to Waterford and Cork which used the deep water harbour here. Opened as Milford Haven on 15 April 1856, it was renamed Neyland in February 1859 and New Milford in November 1859. It became Neyland once again on 30 August 1906.

Passenger services were withdrawn on 15 June 1964 and today the area has been developed as a marina and waterfront homes. The building on the left is the Brunel Arcade with a chandlery, café and restaurant. *GW Trust/Geoff Wright*

Clarbeston Road

'4300' class 2-6-0 No 7320 enters Clarbeston Road on 28 July 1962 with the Neyland portion of the down 'Capitals United Express'. This was the junction station for lines to Fishguard Harbour, Milford Haven and Neyland.

The Neyland branch has now gone, and the main station building has been replaced by a brick shelter. Clarbeston Road is still served by services to and from Fishguard Harbour and Milford Haven. On 18 June 2001, Class 143 No 143603 arrives with the 11.32 request stop service to Haverfordwest. *L. Sandler/Geoff Wright*

Goodwick shed

The Great Western engine shed at Goodwick is depicted here on 19 October 1921. Standing alongside the coaling plant are 'Saint' class 4-6-0 No 2913 *Saint Andrew* and '517' class 0-4-2T No 1161. On the turntable is a 'Bulldog' class 4-4-0. Goodwick was opened by the Great Western in 1906 and closed on 9 September 1963.

The site is now covered by the Goodwick Industrial Estate and can be seen in this picture taken from the overbridge on 18 June 2001.
GW Trust/Geoff Wright

Fishguard Harbour

This excellent view shows Fishguard Harbour on 28 August 1963. Harbour station was opened by the Great Western on 30 August 1906, with through boat trains to and from Paddington.

Viewed from the same spot on 18 June 2001, the station has been reduced to one platform. The site of the old sheds and warehouses is now a trailer park. In the harbour is the Stena roll-on roll-off ferry service to Rosslare. *R. Stark/Geoff Wright*

Abermule

A down train arrives at Abermule hauled by a Cambrian Railways 4-4-0 in circa 1910. Standing in the bay is a Kerry branch service. On 26 January 1921, a mix-up whilst exchanging tablets resulted in the local stopping service colliding head-on with the express service from Aberystwyth, about one mile west of the station; 17 people were killed. The station was closed to passengers on 14 June 1965.

Pictured here on 20 July 2001, part of the up platform still remains, but all traces of the down platform and Kerry branch bay, which closed to passengers on 9 February 1931, have now gone. *GW Trust/Peter Heath*

Caersws

Caersws station and level crossing, pictured here on 2 August 1950, was situated on the Cambrian main line just west of Moat Lane Junction. The station is still open for passengers, but goods services were withdrawn on 4 May 1964.

Today, the signal has gone but little has changed; this view is dated 16 July 2001. The station is now an unstaffed halt and services stop on request. The small signalbox controls the crossing. *GW Trust/David Heath*

Llanbrynmair

This post-1923 picture shows the main building at Llanbrynmair station on the Cambrian main line. Two of the posters can be read through a magnifier and are Great Western, advertising an express service to the Cambrian Coast and trips to Llangollen. The station was interesting as the platform was bisected by a level crossing. It was closed on 14 June 1965, while goods traffic had been withdrawn a year earlier.

Barmouth Junction

Having just crossed Barmouth Bridge
'4300' class 2-6-0 No 7313 approaches
Barmouth Junction with a Pwllheli to
Birmingham via Ruabon service on
1 September 1958. The Ruabon to
Barmouth line was closed to passengers
on 18 January 1965.

Approaching the end of the one
surviving platform on 16 July 2001 is
Class 158 No 158856 forming the 14.58
Central Trains service from Pwllheli to
Machynlleth. Barmouth Junction was
renamed Morfa Mawddach on 13 June
1960. *GW Trust/David Heath*

Today, the building, which shows little
change, is in use as a private residence.
The British Railways sign in the centre
advertises the Ffestiniog Railway;
photographed on 16 July 2001.
GW Trust/Peter Heath

251

Barmouth

This undated view shows an ex-Cambrian Railways 'Large Goods' class 0-6-0 No 884 passing through Barmouth with an up goods service. Built by Neilson, Reid in January 1899 as Cambrian No 87, it was withdrawn from service in August 1947.

The same spot on 16 July 2001 with Class 158 No 158845 leaving with the 08.00 Central Trains service from Pwllheli to Birmingham. Both up and down platforms are still in use, but the up bay platform, seen in the first picture, was closed in 1965 and has since been removed. The signalbox, which also controlled the adjacent level crossing, was closed on 22 October 1988. *GW Trust/Peter Heath*

Portmadoc

The up 'Cambrian Coast Express', the 9.55am service from Pwllheli to Paddington, hauled by 'Manor' class 4-6-0 No 7806 *Cockington Manor* and 'Dukedog' 4-4-0 No 9017, wait at Portmadoc on 1 September 1958.

Class 156 No 156417 arrives at what is now Porthmadog station with the 14.48 Central Trains service from Pwllheli to Machynlleth on 18 July 2001. Part of the old station building has been converted into the Station Inn — a pub on the platform. *GW Trust/David Heath*

Afon Wen

Looking down from the footbridge as '2251' class 0-6-0 No 2287 runs through Afon Wen on 1 September 1958, having arrived with the up 'Welshman' service from Pwllheli. This was the junction for the ex-LNWR branch from Caernarvon, which joined the Cambrian line just beyond the station, on the right. The 'Welshman' was a summer-only service from Euston to Pwllheli and Portmadoc via the North Wales coast and split into two portions at this point. Afon Wen was closed to passengers on 7 December 1964.

The remains of the up platform can still be seen as Class 156 No 156417, in old Regional Railways livery, passes with the 12.53 service from Aberystwyth to Pwllheli on 19 July 2001. *GW Trust/Peter Heath*

Pwllheli

An early postcard view of the station entrance and harbour at Pwllheli.

A similar high-level view was not available on 18 July 2001, but the entrance to the single platform here has now been moved to the side of the building. The main building has been restored and is in current use as the Station Café. *GW Trust/David Heath*

Pwllheli

Pwllheli was the northern terminus of the Cambrian Railways and was opened by the Aberystwyth & Welsh Coast Railway on 10 October 1867. On 1 September 1958, '2251' class 0-6-0 No 2287 waits to leave Platform 1 with the Pwllheli portion of the up 'Welshman' service to Euston.

Much of the station area is now in commercial use, and the site of the platform now forms part of the station car park. On 18 July 2001, Class 156 No 156444 waits to leave with the 16.45 service to Machynlleth.
GW Trust/Peter Heath

List of Locations